How to Succeed in the Police Recruitment Process

Even if you have no idea where to start with your preparation

BRENDAN O'BRIEN

HOW TO SUCCEED IN THE POLICE RECRUITMENT PROCESS

Copyright @ 2021. Brendan O'Brien. All rights reserved. No part of this book may be reproduced by any mechanical, photographic, or electronic process, or in the form of a phonographic recording; nor may it be stored in a retrieval system, transmitted, or otherwise be copied for public or private use other than for "fair use" as brief quotations embodied in articles and reviews without prior written permission of the publisher.

This publication is designed to provide accurate and authoritative information regarding the subject matter covered. It is sold with the understanding that the publisher is not engaged in rendering legal, accounting, or other professional services. If you require legal advice or other Human Resources expert assistance, you should seek the services of a competent professional.

Design and cover art by NOiSE Creative York

Disclaimer: The author makes no guarantees to the results you'll achieve by reading this book. The Police Recruitment Process requires dedication and hard work. The results and client case studies presented in this book represent results achieved working directly with the author. Your results may vary when undertaking the Police Recruitment Process on your own.

ISBN: 9798489237727

TABLE OF CONTENTS

6	Introduction
16	What can the Police Service offer me?
21	The practical stuff – Qualifications required for you to join and other practical considerations
29	Qualifications, Skills, Experience and how to conduct your own 'Values and Skills Audit'
41	'Plugging In' - Developing your Police DNA!
51	Overview of the Police Recruitment Process
60	The Application Form
72	Common Application Form Mistakes and How to Avoid Them
85	Values, Corporate Knowledge and Awareness. The Impact of Being a Police Officer on Your Personal Life
95	Situational Judgement Tests
102	Stage 2 of the Online Assessment Centre
120	The Online Assessment Centre Stage 3 Written Exercise
139	The Online Assessment Centre Stage 3 Briefing Exercise
150	Introduction to your Final Interview / In-Force Interview / Senior Interview
158	Your motivation and inspiration to join the Police Service – exploring your 'Why?'
166	How to structure your Competency and Values Interview Answers
179	How to answer 'Forward Facing' questions
185	Sample Final Interview Questions!
195	Direct Entry Detective Assessments
206	Conclusion

BRENDAN O'BRIEN

Introduction

The first step toward your journey in becoming a Police Officer
Hey, folks! Brendan here from Bluelight. Welcome to:
'How to Succeed in the Police Recruitment Process, even if you have no idea where to start with your preparation!'

This is your welcome chapter to the book. It's the first part, the first step toward your journey in becoming a Police Officer by passing everything the first time around.

That's what we're after!

So, I'm really, really excited about this, and I hope you are too. By following everything that I'm going to talk about and show you, you can pretty much guarantee that you are going to succeed in your police recruitment journey.

So, pay attention to everything that I'm going to tell you!

This book is a result of so many of you who have been successful already. All of those 'Bluelighters' out there who have been successful already - over 10,000 of you!

So many of you over the years have been asking me, 'Brendan, you should do a book on Police Recruitment.' But one of the things that has held me back is the fact that, as soon as you publish a book on Police Recruitment, it's out of date because things are changing all the time. I spend all my time obsessing about those changes in the Police Recruitment process, so I can ensure that you're going to be successful in your journey.

I'll be introducing you to interview skills. I will provide you with guidance on how to approach new types of interviews, and I'll be introducing you to the techniques required to pass the Online Assessment Centre. I'm all over it like a rash to make sure I provide you with a structured approach that's going to enable you to pass first time.

Something else about this book you should know – most authors write a book and then publish an audio version of them reading it. I tried going down that road but found that what I was writing was a bit stuffy and boring. So, I decided to do the audio version first and then have it transcribed! As a result, the style of this book might come across as if you were listening to me talking – conversational and quite informal, exactly what I wanted the contents to be!

Just in case you're thinking, 'Who is this Brendan guy?' 'Where does he come from?' 'What has he been doing so I should actually listen to him?' Well, in 1985, I went through the Police Recruitment process, just like you are now. Can I share what it involved with you? It was one of the most gruelling processes as I've ever been through. Why gruelling? Well, because it wasn't just about interviews and assessment centres. They took us to the Welsh mountains!

This was for the Cheshire Constabulary, a total of six days' worth of interviews and assessments, and a lot of it was physical. Three days and two nights of those six days were spent in the Welsh mountains where they 'beasted' us: running / climbing up and down mountains; crossing fast-flowing rivers; falling off oil drums, backward and blindfolded at 11 o'clock at night - all sorts of weird stuff. I thought I was joining the Royal Marines not the police service! But I passed it, and I passed the final interview and I started on the police in September 1985. Now, how did I manage to get through everything the first time as a 20-year-old? How did I manage to get through everything first time? Well, I had someone like me who was helping to support me through the process. He'd not been a police officer before - this was one of my friend's father, he was really wise, and he knew exactly the approaches I should take to deal with conundrums and problems in my life. Although indirectly, he helped me prepare for all the different exercises that I was expecting or even the ones I wasn't expecting.

So, Vincent, thank you very much for all your support over the years in helping me to become an analytical decision maker and someone who thought carefully about what the right thing to do was, ahead of time, even if no-one was watching. That's called Integrity. I hope you are resting in peace, wherever you are.

So, this book is dedicated to Vincent as a way of thanking him for all the deep conversations we had all those years ago. Vincent really helped me, guided me through some interesting and difficult times. I know you might be having these now because when you're in your teens or early 20s, and you're thinking, 'what next? What am I going to do? What's going to be my future?' The answers aren't always obvious. Actually, forget teens or early 20's, that could be you any age!

Well, I was fortunate. I got that position in the police first time and ever since then, it's just been awesome. What an awesome Journey.

From 1985, I spent four years in the Cheshire Constabulary, and then, I went to Bermuda, where I ended up as a detective within Special Branch. After three years there I went to Greater Manchester and got promoted to Sergeant very quickly. I'd already passed the Sergeant's exam and went on to succeed in taking on a whole lot of roles. They were mostly operational, but I also spent some time in police training. That's where I got really interested in personnel evaluation systems, things like The College of Policing Competency and Values Framework.

I went back to university and studied for a Master's in Education, where I focused on personnel evaluation systems. I became an NVQ Assessor, NVQ Internal Verifier. I did a lot of work nationally with what is now Skills for Justice on standards, qualifications, and assessment systems.

Some of the work I did in 2000 has eventually resulted in things like The Competency and Values Framework. So, if you want to blame anyone for the Competency and Values Framework, here I am!
From there I became an Inspector in Neighbourhood Policing for eight years. I've also been a Staff Officer for Chief Officers and have spent a lot of time back on response. For my last year of service, I was in the Strategic Change Branch focusing on Community Engagement and Problem Solving

What an awesome career!

Since I've retired, I've been coaching and supporting people to succeed in the police recruitment process. Over 10,000 people have succeeded because of my support.

I've also been doing other work. I spent three years with the European Union on the International Advisory Board for a big project looking at improving community policing. I've done a lot of work with police forces and councils improving their problem-solving capability, spoken at conferences about community engagement and problem-solving. Honestly, post-retirement is just as awesome as being in the police.

So, that's a little bit about me. This is why you should listen to me! However, I've not always had a successful ride.

Back in, let's see, it was about 1998, I started getting cocky. I started thinking, 'Hey, I can walk any interview!'
I went for two interviews for national positions, and both were absolute train wrecks! They were awful! I remember the Chief Inspector's face looking at me when I delivered some of the answers – I know he was thinking, 'what on Earth was that?'
I swore this was never going to happen again. The thing is, I took all the advice, the advice that you're probably hearing now. Things like, 'just act naturally, just be yourself and you'll be fine.' 'Just act naturally. Just be yourself. Just answer the questions honestly.' Well, I answered all the questions honestly. I acted naturally. I was myself, but I wasn't prepared, and wasn't delivering a structured and detailed approach that was authentic and emotional. I didn't know what I was being assessed against. I'd not done my homework. I'd not practiced. I'd not prepared. As a result of that, I failed at both of those interviews. I swore that was never going to happen again.

I was already doing my Masters in Education and I thought this is an ideal opportunity to start developing systems and processes that would work for me in the future, and they did. They also worked for those people who I helped as well. A lot of people who I helped in force, a lot of my colleagues who got promoted to Sergeant, to Inspector, and who succeeded in getting specialist positions.

So, this is something I've been doing now for, well, over 20 years. Let's see now. Yeah, it's going to be over 25 years, a quarter of a century! So, I've been doing this for a long time, so you're in safe hands. That's what I'm trying to say. You're in safe hands.

So, what are we going to cover in this in this book?

Well, first, we're going to look at the police. I'm not going to tell you all about the police. I'm going to tell you what you should be researching to find out more about the police.

This is the ethos behind what I do - I will show you the way but you've got to do the hard work.

The police don't owe you a living. Let's just get that straight. They don't owe you a living.

You're going to have to work hard to earn the right to have that warrant card in your pocket, to earn the right to be one of Her Majesty's servants. Did you know that when you became a police officer, you're not actually employed by anyone? The Chief Constable doesn't employ you. The Mayor doesn't employ you. The Policing and Crime Commissioner doesn't employ you. You are not formally employed. You are a servant of a Majesty, The Queen. You are a Crown Servant, what a special position that is. That's just incredible, isn't it?

I'm going to talk to you in the next chapter about what you need to do to start building up your 'Police DNA' so that you can just plugin. Once you join, you can just plugin, and it also makes it easier for your interviews as well, because you know the context of the answers that you're giving. You know how they can get be contextualized into the world of policing. So, that's what one of the first chapters is going to be about.

Then, we're going to look at self-assessment before you even do things like application forms. We're going to do a self-assessment, we're going to do a little bit of work around the Competency and Values Framework to see what values and behaviours you need to improve on to ensure that your application form gets through the first time.

Remember, the purpose of the application form when you do apply is just to get you an assessment centre or an interview. It serves no other purpose. This is how forces screen thousands of people out. I'm going to make sure the work you do now will prepare you for your application form in several months' time or in a year's time, whenever it may be. The time to start preparing is now. Not what a lot of people do, which is they apply for the police and then they look backward thinking, 'what examples can I use about decision-making? What examples can I use about problem-solving? What examples can use about working collaboratively with others? Oh, no! I've never challenged anyone's inappropriate behaviour!'

That's where they struggle, because of not preparing and they have not been pushing themselves and giving 120% without being asked to do so against the values and behaviours required by The Competency and Values Framework.

We're going to do a little bit of work around self-assessment. Then, we're going to look at what things you should be doing to gain the right experience. We're also going to look at why the Special Constabulary probably isn't the best idea, although they may be so many people around you saying, 'join the Special Constabulary. That will give you loads of opportunities to demonstrate your capability as a future Police Officer.'

No, it won't actually, and it's not going to make much difference to your recruitment journey.

If anything, I'm going to share with you in that chapter why being a Special Constable might be detrimental to your police recruitment journey. We'll look at the other things that you should be doing that are going to be faster than joining the Special Constabulary.

I'm going to look at what the police offer you because it is an awesome career. If you give a lot, they can give you a lot back. So, that's going to be the next chapter.

Moving on from there, making sure that you comply with all the eligibility rules, because so many of you get through all the recruitment processes, you're successful at the assessment centre, you're successful at the interview, and then you get all the way to the end and find that you're not eligible to join that force. But you might have been eligible to join another force, or you just find that you are just not eligible full stop and you've done all that work only to get heartbroken right at the very end of it. So, I'm going to talk to you about that. That's really important. Forces leave the eligibility checks until the end, bizarrely. That's just what they do.

Then, we're going to take a look at the qualifications and the experience that they're looking for that will build upon that self-assessment work, making sure you've got the right qualifications to join the service, the police force that you want to join. There are 43 Home Office forces out there, and then, we've got Police Scotland, Police Service of Northern Ireland, Ministry of Defence Police, Civil Nuclear Constabulary, all the small forces like Ports of Belfast Police, ones you didn't even know they existed. Then, we've got States of Jersey, Guernsey, and Isle of Man Police.

There are so many police forces out there that you can join. Some of them might require you some residency conditions and they all have different qualifications requirements. They all have different requirements, some things like maximum points on a driving licence you can have, some are 6 points, while others are 9 points. Do you even have to have a driving licence? I'm going to go through all of that because that's really important.

What we're going to look at, as well, after that. We're going to look at the application form, what the actual process involves, making sure that you really clued up about what's going to happen at every stage and what you can start doing to prepare for each stage.

We'll take a look at the application form, then we're going to look at what you should be doing to prepare for the assessment centre.

HOW TO SUCCEED IN THE POLICE RECRUITMENT PROCESS

The next chapter will be looking at the In-Force interview, all the different things that can occur in the police interview, all the different types of questions that you could get asked, looking at the impact of being a police officer, some of the challenges that you are going to face as a Police Officer and how you can react to them.

Moving on from there, we're going to take a look at how to make sure that you secure an earlier intake date rather than what some people are getting, which is a probable start date which is two years away. So, they've already spent a year in the recruitment process, and then they're getting given a probable start date that's two years away! You can avoid that and I'm going to show you how.

Then, we're going to take a look at (we're almost at the end now!) all the different routes that you can take to join the police such as Direct Entry Detective and Firearms Officer, and who knows, by the time we get to that chapter, there may be one or two more different ways. Also, things like Direct Entry Inspector, Direct Entry Superintendent (but they're starting to fall out of favour a little bit).

So, a whole of the stuff is going to get covered. Interspersed throughout the book I'm also going to answer some of the frequently asked questions that people tend to ask in the awesome Bluelight Facebook group. This is a community of almost 20,000 members - people who have got a shared interest in police recruitment and joining the police. Over the years, so many questions get asked, and they tend to be the same questions.

So, what do you think, folks? Are you excited? Oh, my goodness, I'm so excited to be sharing all my knowledge, my understanding, and my practical experience with you throughout the course of this book. It just going to be awesome. I can't wait. Please remember, at any time, if you're confused about anything, or you're not sure about anything, just reach out to me, info@bluelightconsultancy.com, and I'll be there at the other end to answer any questions that you might have. Or if you're in the Facebook group, you'll see me posting in there all the time. You can always contact me via messenger.

To access the Facebook Group as well as my YouTube channel, Podcasts, Twitter, and a host of resources such as question banks, Masterclass Webinars, and massive discounts with bonuses you won't find anywhere else on my courses, especially those courses that involve interactive practice with me, then go to the 'Offer Wall' at the end of every chapter.

So, are you excited about the next chapter? Where we're going to take a look at the police and look at what you need to do to ensure that the Police is in your DNA?

https://bluelightonline.co.uk/book

Chapter 1 - What can the Police Service offer me?

In this chapter you are going to start your recruitment journey by looking at what the police service can offer you in terms of very practical things, things like pay, pensions and career opportunities.

First, I'm going to look at the starting salary. It's changed a lot over the years and the salary ladder has now been compressed a little bit. It used to be 0 to 15 years, now, it is 0 to 7 years, which means after your first 7 years, you could be earning a very healthy salary. What I'd like you to do is to check on the entry-level salaries for your force because it can vary from force to force. This might influence your decision to join where you're living now or maybe one of the neighbouring forces or perhaps a force right across the other end of the country.

I know some forces will offer the same starting salary no matter what route you go in, whether it's a degree holder or the policing degree holder or the police constable degree apprenticeship. They will pay the same starting salary, and at the time of writing this book, it's in the region of about £24,000. However, for other forces, for the police constable degree apprenticeship, they pay far less, anything from £19,000 plus.

So that's something to watch out for. It's not the same across all forces and although there is guidance on pay and conditions, in terms of your pay and the starting point, it's up to the force what point they start you on. This will rise in the first 7 years or so to a salary of about £42,000, which is very, very respectable. If you think about it, if you join aged 18 or 19, then by the time you're 26, 27, you could be on a salary in the £40,000 plus bracket, which is pretty good. There's also the opportunity to go for the rank of sergeant or inspector.

So, if you really set your stall out, there's no reason why you can be a sergeant or an inspector by the time you're 30 if you joined at the age of 18 / 19. Being a sergeant or inspector has got nothing to do with your age - it's got everything to do with your experience and your capability, your values, and your skills. So, this is something you might want to start thinking about very early stage of your career.

The other thing the service also offers is an awesome pension, an absolutely awesome pension. You will be enrolled automatically, but you can opt out. What I would advise you to do though, is to stay in it, no matter how much of a big chunk you think is coming out of your salary every month, and it is a big chunk. But because it's a big chunk of your salary that's going to come out, it will pay off at the other end, because although the pension has changed over the years, it is still unbeatable.

You won't find a pension anywhere like it on the High Street. So please, my advice to you is, if you possibly can stick with it, even if it means a diet of beans on toast. All right, I'm joking there, you can't survive on a diet of beans on toast, but you get my jist. It's worth contributing into, even though at an age in your twenties. You may be thinking, 'oh, that's miles off.' But look, I'm at the other end as a retired officer, and I'm so glad that I contributed for every year that I could because it's paid off at this end where I am now enjoying a very healthy police pension. I've invested in it, I've worked hard for it, I absolutely deserve it, but if I had opted out, then my pension would be very, very different, so please do stick with it.

You're going to get a lot of opportunities to develop yourself into so many specialist roles or ranks, but remember those opportunities are exactly that, you've got to seize them.

HOW TO SUCCEED IN THE POLICE RECRUITMENT PROCESS

Your initial training will be provided for you, and once you're out of your student officer period, which typically is three years long, although it could be less if you're a degree holder, then there are so many opportunities for you. Whether it's Road Policing Unit, Tactical Aid Unit, Specialist Operations, Firearms, Dog Handler, being a detective, there are so many careers within careers within the Police Service.

That's the one thing that I benefited from all the way through my career - all the different careers within careers. I got to serve in three different forces (Cheshire, Bermuda and GMP), got to work as part of a Home Office Department, and served in so many different roles: from Training, Special Branch, Staff Officer, Custody Officer to Neighbourhood Policing, and it was all by choice - my choice.

It's your choice whether you want to go into those departments, and your choice as to whether you go for promotion. A lot of the positions you might aspire to are hotly contested so you do need to set your stall out at the earliest opportunity, especially for popular roles like dog handler. The career opportunities are absolutely amazing, second to none, but they are opportunities like I said, and you've got to set your stall out to seize those opportunities.

None of this will happen by 'happy accident.' It will only happen by design. So more about that once you're in the police, because we do have a lot of services which provide for serving officers to help them develop their most awesome, successful, and fulfilling careers.

You're also going to find some really good support for the times when you may struggle in terms of your mental health and your physical well-being. There's a wide range of services available, and you'll also find the Police Federation offer a lot of that kind of support also. Please do choose to join the Police Federation because as well as offering you personal support, they also have a legal scheme, which can be really helpful for you if you ever need it.

If you ever find yourself at the receiving end of a complaint that's unjustified The Police Federation will fight your corner for you and provide those legal services, but only if you are a fully paid-up member of the Police Federation. So, I'd advise you to join them.

There are also going to be various staff support groups available for you, from LGBT groups to Black Police Officers Association, as well as lots of sporting opportunities.

Depending on the force, they'll be the likes of rugby teams, cricket, football, and hockey teams. And if there's not a team for you, then start one! There are so many of my colleagues who started off small divisional clubs, some of them went on to become force-wide. As an example, one of my fellow sergeants set up a sailing team, a sailing squad on division, and then that later became a force-wide club.

There are plenty of opportunities for you to get involved in sports and hobbies. Depending on the force, they should also have some facilities for you to utilise, like a police rugby ground or football pitch. It depends on the force because Austerity did strip away some of those facilities.

So, excellent facilities for you, superb opportunities, so many careers within careers, but those are just some of the things that the police service will offer you. But the one thing to remember is, how the service will also offer you something which is difficult to describe, they'll give you this incredible opportunity to develop a successful career. But one that's not that's not just successful, but deeply fulfilling. There is a difference here because you can have a successful career but if it's not fulfilling, then it can feel a bit empty.

How many people do you know who talk about how much they love their job? How many people do you know say things like, 'it's the best job in the world?' Or, 'I wouldn't have done anything else.' Now, this is something that's quite unique to policing, because although police officers do like to have a grumble and groan about the service every now and then, what they do have in common is that they will, in general, describe the job as, 'the best one in the world' and seriously it is. If I had my time again, I'd do exactly the same thing.

What the Police Service does offer you is all those practical things (pay, pension etc) plus this opportunity to have a career which is deeply, deeply fulfilling. Where you'll have opportunities to help change people's lives for the good and help communities become the best versions of themselves. There really is nothing like it.

So hopefully, you've got something out of this chapter, folks. It's quite a short one, but I just thought I'd add this chapter at the start to ensure you have got a really good feel for the practical things that the police will offer you. Plus, that one thing that a lot of police forces when they're advertising and marketing for new recruits tend not to describe, and that's a fulfilling, a deeply fulfilling career.

https://bluelightonline.co.uk/book

Chapter 2 - The practical stuff – Qualifications required for you to join and other practical considerations

In this chapter, I'm going to cover very practical elements of you joining the police, which are all the practical eligibility requirements. Now please, do take note of these criteria. So many people, so many of my clients, have got all the way through the recruitment process, only to face disappointment at the end as they do not meet the essential criteria. The end of the recruitment journey could have been a 12-18 months, sometimes two-year-long journey, only for them to find out that they passed everything, but they're not eligible for one of the reasons that I'm going to outline here.

Now, this list is far from exclusive, there may be other things that you're Force chooses to add. But these are some of the main eligibility criteria – I'm also going to comment on some of the things that people slip up on, to make sure you don't fall into any of the traps.

Now I'm not talking about educational qualifications here. That's the subject of another chapter. These are just some of the more practical elements. So, the first big one, and this is a big and recent change, is the age you must be to apply to join as a police officer. A lot of you may have thought you had to be 18 and a half to apply to join the police. This changed recently, now you must be 17 or over to apply. So, on your 17th birthday, you could apply to join the police!

You may be thinking that it's far too young? Well, it's not. I joined the police when I was 20. And 18 or 20, it doesn't really matter. I was young and, in many respects, quite naive as well. But I still made a good career out of it. So, it's not about age, it's more about your attitude towards the profession, towards this career, this awesome job of being a police officer. The recruitment process is all about your attitude, your values, and your previous life experience.

HOW TO SUCCEED IN THE POLICE RECRUITMENT PROCESS

You may also be thinking, 'how am I going to get life experience at 17?' Well, think about things like this you can write about in your application form, or talk about at your interview: Scouting; Guiding; the organisations that you've been part of at school; sporting events; part-time jobs. They all provide plenty of opportunities for you to get the sort of experience that the police are looking for. And if you have the right qualities, they will recruit you at 18. It's an urban myth that they will discount your application until you are in your 20s.

So many of my clients have succeeded at the age of 18. Remember, you can apply at 17, but you must be 18 when you're appointed. But that's not really a problem. If you've got your sights set on being a police officer, there's no reason why you shouldn't be applying at age 17. On the day of your birthday, get the application in, straight away because it's going to take a year or more for you to go through the recruitment process.

There's also another age limit I need to mention, and this is the one for those of you who are getting a little bit more 'respectful' in your years. So, once you're in your 50s, there's a point at which they won't recruit you anymore, and there's no point in applying. Because the retirement age for police constables and sergeants is 60 years old, they want to get their money's worth out of you. Depending on the Force, they may say that you must be 57 to apply or even 56. They don't want to recruit you at 58 and a half as you will only be with them for 18 months service and for all that time you will a student officer. And then you're going to have to go because the upper retirement ages 60. So be careful of that.

Another thing you might be thinking is, 'am I going to get discriminated against because of my age? Because I'm older than most recruits?' The truth is, absolutely not. So many of my clients have managed to succeed in the police recruitment process who have been in their 50's.

One of my clients was 57 years old. He came to me and said, 'I've got this one opportunity to join the Metropolitan Police.' He didn't need to work; he was already a millionaire. He'd been in the Military, achieved a very respectful rank, retired, set his own business up, sold it for a lot of money, played golf a little bit, then set up another business, and sold that one for a lot of money. He came to me saying, 'look, my childhood dream is to be a police officer. Could you help me achieve it?' And there he was, he got in. He got in touch with me when he retired at 60 to thank me. He'd had an awesome couple of years in the police. It kind of amused him a little bit to think how even got a police pension. This was someone who just didn't need the pension at all. But I know for many of you, you don't fall into that bracket, do you? What mattered was how at 57 he achieved his childhood dream – if you are in your late 40's or 50's, that could be you!

Another important criteria you must comply with, is to have three years of continuous residency in the United Kingdom at the point of submitting your application. This is one they're quite strict about and if you've been traveling, then you could fall foul of this. I do know people who have worked on cruise ships or who have had working visa abroad who have fallen foul of this. If you've been serving Her Majesty's Armed Forces outside of the UK, this does not apply to you. But if you fall into any other residency criteria category, it absolutely does. So, you've got to have those three years of continuous residency in the UK at the point of applying.

Now, if you've gone traveling for four to six months, I'd say that's just an extended holiday. But check with the Force that you're applying to, because if you've certainly been out of the country for over a year then that could well be an issue.

You must also be a UK, EU, or Commonwealth Citizen, and you must have no restrictions at all on your stay in the UK. You've got to have a leave to remain and if you're an EU citizen, you've got to have all the appropriate registrations to ensure that you have no restrictions, whatsoever, on your stay in the UK.

HOW TO SUCCEED IN THE POLICE RECRUITMENT PROCESS

Some Forces will require you to have a full UK driving licence. Some don't, but most do. And you must not have 9 or more penalty points on your licence (for some forces this is 6 points). If you do need a driving licence, you can't have more than 9 points on your licence at the point of applying or any point throughout the process. That's important because if there's any changes to your status you must tell the Force. Especially, if it involves things like more points on your licence, which would lead to a mandatory disqualification.

The things you can't be as a police officer, or at any time before you apply. You cannot be a member of an extreme political organisation such as the British National Party, National Front, or Combat 18, or any other banned institution. Not banned in the country, because as a citizen, you can be a member of the British National Party, you can be a member of the National Front and you can be a member of Combat 18. But if you are or have been a member of any of those organisations, you will not get into the police. You'll have to declare as well, whether you have been or are currently a member of any of those organisations. If you have been and you declare that you haven't, you will be found out and they will fail your application on the grounds of integrity. If they find out once you have joined, you will be arrested, prosecuted, and dismissed from the service.

Next, we come to tattoos. Different forces have different policies on this. There is a national policy on tattoos, but it is very woolly, it's very vague. However, a lot of Forces try to maintain it very strictly. So, for some forces, if you have any visible tattoos, they won't accept you. Some Forces will accept you if you've got tattoos on your forearm, but they may put a condition on you joining, saying that you must always wear a long sleeve shirt. However, you'll find how that gets relaxed once you've in the job, as no one out on the frontline will care, including your bosses.

However, tattoos on your neck, face, and hands, they can be a problem. But not for every individual. I do know of some individuals in some Forces, who managed to get in with tattoos on their neck, face, or hands. But they will be judged on their merits or otherwise. And this will involve you having to take photographs of those tattoos and send them in. My advice, because so many people ask this in the Bluelight Facebook Group, 'I'm in the recruitment process and I'm thinking about getting a tattoo. Should I?' My advice always is no, don't, just don't. Don't get a tattoo if you're in the recruitment process, wait until you've got that warrant card in your pocket, and then get a tattoo. Because you'll find that they're a lot more relaxed in respect of tattoos and the tattoo policy once you're in the police. And, because it's about the sort of tattoo you've got as well. Tattoos of things like skulls and crossbones are a big No-No.

However, there can also be misunderstandings about what tattoos mean. Here is a case in point - I do know of one individual who had a dagger on the calf of his leg. So, no-one's ever going to see the calf of his legs anyway, but he had a dagger on the calf of his leg, and his application was initially refused because of this. But this wasn't just a dagger, it was the emblem of the Royal Marines and he had been a Royal Marine. He did appeal it and he did succeed in his appeal, because the individuals who first viewed the tattoo didn't know of its relevance, they didn't know the context. So, this is something else that's really important - don't just send in a photograph of your tattoo, describe its relevance, so they can understand why you have that tattoo or why it is so important to you.

This next criteria is really important. You must not have any convictions or recent cautions, bind overs or findings of guilt. Now, the attitude towards accepting people who may have had a caution earlier on in their life aged 14 can vary from force to force. Let's say you had a caution for, I don't know, smashing bottles against a bus stop and it broke one of the bus stop windows, something like that. You may get in with this. But equally, you might not do. I know I'm being a bit vague here, but when it comes to things like child cautions, adult cautions, convictions, there is a national policy, but it's the interpretation of that policy that differs from force to force.

If you Google 'National Police Vetting Criminal Convictions,' it will bring up the PDF of the latest guidance. Some offences, whether you committed them when you're 14, 22 or 42 mean you are never going to get in. It may surprise you that one of those is something as simple as shoplifting. The offence of shoplifting, by the way, is theft. So, if you committed an offence of theft, aged 15, and the theft was of £1 worth of sweets, you may find that that could be a bar to join in the police forever. Why? Because the offence of theft involves dishonesty, and any offence, that has any link with dishonesty, is going to be an automatic failure. So, you need to be really careful there. If you are that younger age and you are reading this, be careful about what you do, because you could find it ruins your dream of becoming a police officer.

However, just because you do have a conviction or a caution doesn't mean to say you can't be a police officer, but it can get complicated. It can involve you having to wait 10-15 years before you can reapply again. Do check the policy, it's really important to make sure that you comply with it.

As part of your vetting the force might ask you a question like, 'have you had any police contact?' if they do, it is so important to list all police contact you've had. If they ask you for any convictions or any cautions or bind overs, then I'd do the same thing. I would list all police contact that I've had and the circumstances behind it. I'd go really over-the-top there and declare as much as you possibly can for the vetting unit to decide whether you are being as honest as you can be. Because if they find that you haven't declared something when you knew about it, they will fail you on integrity.

One of my clients fell foul of this because he had a bind over for a breach of the peace from about 20 something years before. It was a difficult time in his life, he was splitting up with his wife, and he couldn't remember the exact year, so he gave an approximate year. They failed him on that, they failed him because he wasn't being precise enough with the year. What they said was, 'you're not being as honest as you can be with us.' I thought that was a little bit over the top and so did he. On my advice, he applied to another force who had a far more common-sense approach, and they accepted them and he's now police officer.

Moving on from convictions, you can't have any current County Court Judgments (CCJs) or be declared bankrupt. You can only apply if it's been three years since the date of your debts were discharged, so with a CCJ or bankruptcy, you can apply, but you must wait until three years since the date your debts were discharged.

Some forces will tell you that you can't apply to join the Police within six months of failing a College of Policing Assessment Centre. That's a little bit more fluid now and you may find that some Forces tell you it's three months. If you have failed in assessment centre before, do check with the Force that you want to apply to, because you may find that you don't have to wait six months, you only have to wait for three months.

Another thing that forces often tell you is that you can't have an ongoing application with any other force in England and Wales. They'll tell you things like how this is in accordance with National Recruitment Policy. However, the National Recruitment Policy has changed, but a lot of Forces haven't updated their policy. You can apply for as many Forces as you want, but you can only do one College of Policing Assessment within any six-month period.

If you want advice about that, and if you're one of my clients, I'm quite happy to give you the advice that you're looking for, because it can become a bone of contention with some Forces who will say, 'no, you can only apply for one Force.' I've helped more than several of my clients through that before by telling them what to write in their email of appeal, and by giving them the screenshots of the National Policy. One Force did change their policy on the day they were challenged. The Deputy Chief Constable got involved and changed that policy on that day, so good for that Force.

So, folks, those are some of the very practical eligibility criteria. In a separate chapter, I'm going to look at the qualifications, skills, and experience they're looking for in more depth, because it's another subject. I'm not going to say, 'I hope you enjoyed this chapter' because it's very factual, it's very fact-based and it's not really something that you're here to enjoy, but I'd like you to please, pay attention to everything I've said here. Like I said earlier, you'll could get all the way to the end of the recruitment process, only to find that you are not eligible and that can be heart-breaking. Especially as you could also have found a way to make sure that you are eligible.

All right, folks. I'll see you at the next chapter, which is all about your qualifications, skills, and experience.

https://bluelightonline.co.uk/book

Chapter 3 - Qualifications, Skills, Experience and how to conduct your own 'Values and Skills Audit'

In this chapter, we're going to take a look at qualifications, skills, and experience. But not in the mechanistic way that your force might present to you. Although we are going to look at that as well - the minimum qualifications and what sort of skills they're looking for. But we're also going to look at how you go about developing the skills, behaviours, and values they are looking for, so that when it comes to the point of application form, and your interview, you are all set, as opposed to doing what most people do, which is the one big mistake most people make. I'll come to that in a moment so that you can avoid that one big mistake.

So let's take a look first at the sort of qualifications you need to be a police officer. These are constantly changing so please forgive me if they have changed since publication.

At this moment in time, to join the police as a constable, you need to have a degree or be prepared to embark on one (using the Police Constable Degree Apprenticeship).

The bulk of you, I suspect, will be joining using the Police Constable Degree Apprenticeship route. You may be thinking that everything would be consistent across all 43 forces in England and Wales. No, they are not. Every force has completely different educational qualification requirements ranging from two GCSEs in Maths and English, that's all Merseyside Police want, so if you want to join Merseyside Police, all you need is two GCSEs in Maths and English, to 180 UCAS points (3 'A' Levels at B Grade).

HOW TO SUCCEED IN THE POLICE RECRUITMENT PROCESS

Bear in mind that's currently, as per today, as per when I'm writing this book, Merseyside may change to 180 UCAS points, which is currently what Northumbria Police want. You may be thinking it's got something to do with the force. Well, it has, but it's got more to do with the university which they've partnered up with. So, Northumbria Police want 180 UCAS points, which is Three B's at 'A' level, but they will also accept life skills - this is where things get a little bit more confusing.

Every force has a completely different take on what life skills are acceptable. So, some forces will ask you to write an essay where you present evidence of the sort of experiences that are required at the level of learning for a degree from your current career. Other forces like Lincolnshire Police, have a variety of specific and different skills requirements, but they make it really clear as to what those skills need to be. So, to be eligible to join Lincolnshire as a police officer you must have two 'A' levels in any subject - it could be in manicuring horses, if there's an 'A' level in that.

If you do not have two 'A' levels you can join with a policing qualification approved by the Skills of Justice, which is the Sector Skills Council for the Justice Sector.

Or currently be serving as a PCSO and have passed your probationary period satisfactorily as a PCSO.

Or that you are a serving special constable and you've acquired independent patrol status.

Or you're a current police staff member in Lincolnshire Police and you've had two years of continued service.

Or you have served with Her Majesty's Armed Forces, for a minimum of two years.

Or you are able to demonstrate sufficient competence in certain languages, in particular, Arabic, Romanian, and Bulgarian, or you are sufficiently competent in communicating in British sign language or Makaton.

So, you can see there that Lincolnshire are completely the opposite of Northumbria, in that they really do define what they mean by 'life skills.' Northumbria and other forces are a little less specific, you've just got to persuade them through the evidence you present to them that you are sufficiently capable, and you've got sufficient skills to be able to join the police through their recruitment process.

So that's the qualifications, skills, and experience that they're looking for. But there's something else you can do in addition to start preparing for the process. One of the things a lot of forces don't mention is the criteria they're going to assess you against when you do apply. The Competency and Values Framework (CVF) is a document produced by The College of Policing - it outlines all the values, behaviours and the competencies required of a police officer or police staff at any rank. Before you continue you might want to search online for 'Police CVF' – download the document and have it next to you for the next part of this chapter.

As you go through the CVF you'll see how it has different levels within it, you need to be looking at Level One. By the way, don't even bother looking at the 'Wheel of Confusion.' You'll know what I mean when you get to it.

So, at this stage, we're just going to take a look at some of the values and some of the competencies that apply to the recruitment process, so that you can start developing yourself against them. Why do this now? So that when it comes to you applying or you facing your first interview, you are not looking back in your life thinking, 'when have I done that, I can't think of an example when I've done....' (whatever it is that they're looking for in the question).

So what we're going to do here is we're going to look at where we want to be as the best candidate that they can find, so we can answer any application form or interview question that relates to the Competency and Values Framework. Now if that's the future, that's where we want to be, we need to look at where we are now, which is probably lacking in a lot of the experience and the values and the behaviours that they're looking for.

Now, let me give you some examples because this will help bring this concept alive. This is something that we really focus on in the Bluelight online courses and also focus on a lot in the 1-2-1's I do, as well as the group interactive webinars. So that's when this concept of preparing in advance comes alive, that's when it starts becoming real for people - when we start going into that kind of depth.

But let me give you some examples now. So, first, you'd need to dig out a copy of the Competency and Values Framework, that's easy to find. If you just go to Google and search for Competency and Values Framework and the word, 'police.' It should bring up the College of Policing Competency and Values Framework. Now, please do read through it, become familiar with it but don't become obsessive about it. You don't need to obsess about it because I obsess about it on your behalf.

The advice you sometimes see in the Bluelight Police Recruitment Facebook Group, when people ask, 'has anyone got any advice to help me join the police?' is often to just, 'know / learn your competencies.' But what does that mean? Just knowing or learning them isn't enough, we need to understand the competencies, the values, and the behaviours, and make them work for us. This enables us to gain experiences intentionally, experiences we can utilise later in an application form or interview.

So, let's bring that to life for you by looking at the value of Impartiality. One of the behaviours described within that value is being able to gather other people's views and opinions so you can understand other people's points of view. What we're going to do now is we're going to grade ourselves, to rate ourselves on a scale of 1 to 10. Where 1 is 'I'm completely ineffective at doing this,' and 10 is, 'I'm an absolute mastermind at this, I'm just awesome, I'm so effective and efficient at this.

You might be thinking, I don't do actually do this, I haven't ever intentionally sought other people's views and opinions so I can better understand their point of view. Well, you would then score yourself as a 1 and then recognise that this is something that you need to do intentionally. To start thinking about your daily experience in the workplace, or volunteering, or in sporting clubs or in any hobbies you take part in with other people.

So how would you rate yourself on a scale of 1 to 10, where 1 is, 'completely ineffective' and 10 is, 'I'm an absolute mastermind at this.' So, if this is something that you do naturally and you're really good at it, you might be a natural 9, in which case it's not something you need to develop. But if you're a 2 or 3, then yes, this is something you need to develop.

Now you need to put yourself in situations where you do need to gather other people's views and opinions so that you can improve yourself against this value. In seeking other people's views and opinions, about a problem, or a challenge, you need to be careful not to put your point of view in the way. You might not agree with other people's views or opinions, but that doesn't make them wrong, nor does it make you right. They've just got a point of view that is different to yours, but what this enables you to do is to make fair and objective decisions. Decisions or recommendations that are impartial. This is the crux of this value. When you gather everyone's views, you gather everyone's opinions and you understand everyone's point of view, then this enables you to make a fair and objective decision about whatever the problem is.

Here's another criteria from Impartiality I want you to assess yourself against. Where 1 is, 'completely ineffective' and 10 is, 'I'm an absolute mastermind, I'm really effective at this.' Do you make fair and objective decisions based on gathering everyone's views, opinions, and trying to understand their point of view? Rate yourself on a scale of 1 to 10, and if you're rating yourself as a two, then this is something which you need to develop. It's time to intentionally put yourself in situations where you need to make fair and objective decisions, ones where you need to collect all the views, opinions of others and information before you can make a decision. I hope I'm making sense?

Next, we're going to take a look at the value of Integrity, where we're going to look at two of the behaviours in this value. The first one is how you do the right thing in challenging situations. This is a common interview question by the way, when you might be asked, 'can you please tell me about a time when you've done the right thing even when doing nothing would have been the easier option?' So, this behaviour is about the extent to which you do the right thing in challenging situations.

What we're looking for here is, are you the sort of person that will face a challenging situation and you'll do the right thing even though other people may do nothing, or they don't want to do anything about it or don't want to get involved? Are you the sort of person that gets stuck in and you do the right thing, which might not be the popular thing, but it's the right thing to do? This is how you demonstrate Integrity.

Integrity is about making difficult decisions even when you don't have to do so and even when no one else is watching you - you do so because it's the right thing to do.

So once again, rate yourself on the scale of 1 to 10, where one is completely ineffective, and 10 is an absolute mastermind at this. So what mark are you giving yourself? Are you the sort of person that pushes yourself to do the right thing in challenging situations? This is not about being popular, it's about doing the right thing. You can see where we're going with this now? How this will prepare you for future application form questions as well as future interview questions.

Another behaviour from the value of Integrity I want you to take a look at is the extent to which you challenge behaviour, attitudes and language which are inappropriate. This might be in the workplace, or it might be with your friends, or it might be in a sporting event. It works best if it's in the workplace and if it's a fellow colleague or a friend or it might be both. For example, someone who's in the workplace, who is also a good friend of yours, they say something that's inappropriate and someone needs to challenge it. That person is you!

Now, on my courses, I talk about what we mean by challenging. It doesn't have to be you saying, 'I need to challenge your behaviour there.' There are more subtle ways of doing this. using things like CUDSAR, which is a non-contact conflict management model. All my clients get to know this model inside and out.

So, we're going to rate ourselves on a scale of 1 to 10, again, from completely ineffective to a 10, which is, I am an absolute mastermind, I'm so effective at this. This is for the extent to which you challenge behaviour, attitudes, and language, which are inappropriate.

For a lot of you, this is something you won't have done. But now is the time to start putting yourself in situations where you will do this. You might be thinking, 'that's going to be really uncomfortable?' You might also be thinking, 'I'm going to be unpopular.' You might also be thinking, 'why do I have to do that?' Well, you want to be a police officer, don't you?

Challenging inappropriate behaviour is the sort of thing that's expected of a police officer by law. It's in The Code of Ethics, which makes it clear that it's your role to challenge other police officers and other members of police staff behaviour when it falls below the required standard. It's not a 'would you, could you please.' It's not policy, it is the law of this land. So, it's something that you need to demonstrate that you're capable of doing.

This is a popular interview question when it comes to the In-force / Final interview, 'can you tell me about a time when you've challenged someone else's behaviour or language, which is inappropriate?' Your example doesn't have to be challenging sexist or racist behaviour (although that would be a strong example), it could be just someone who's cutting corners in the workplace.

One of my recent clients gave a great example the other day when we were practicing interview questions in one of my Interview Webinars. He talked about how he had challenged one of their fellow workers, who also happened to be a friend of theirs, because they were clocking in half an hour late most mornings and they were claiming that half an hour. When they challenged them about their behaviour, what emerged was that individual was going through a very difficult time at home. They were going through a divorce, and they were finding it very, very difficult to manage their childcare needs - they were dropping their child off at school and then trying to get into work on time and they just weren't succeeding.

So, the solution was simple. My client went with the individual whose behaviour was challenged and held their hand metaphorically to see their boss and explained what had been happening. She got a written warning for her actions, but she also got some support from the organisation so that she could clock in half an hour later and work half an hour later into the evening, which she didn't have a problem with.

So, can you see how the challenging inappropriate behaviours is not about getting people the sack? It's not about getting people kicked out of an organisation. Although, that might be one of the results of your behaviour, and like I said, it's not a popularity contest. Doing the right thing and demonstrating integrity can result in others losing their jobs.

So, I hope all of this is making sense? Let's move on now from the values to the competencies. One of the competencies is, 'We Take Ownership.' So, to what extent are you the sort of person who identifies and responds to problems. On a scale of 1 to 10, mark yourself, grade yourself. Are you the sort of person that recognises where they can help others and takes on tasks and responsibilities to do so?

Doing this is something I call, 'Investing in the emotional bank account.' I go into this in a lot more detail on my courses, but basically, are the sort of person who looks out for people who need support and help in an organisation before they need to ask for it? Do you go out of your way to offer to help and support them before they even realise they need help? By doing so, you are investing in their emotional bank account. So, if you ever need help and support from them, it will be willingly given because you're the one that came to help them before they even knew they needed to ask for that help. So, to what extent on the scale of 1 to 10 again are you that sort of person? Is this something you need to develop?

Now let's look at one more competency. There are more of them of course, I go into this side of your preparation in far, far more depth on my courses, and especially in my interactive webinars. The last competency I'll take a look with you is, 'Deliver, Support and Inspire.' This competency is worded in such a way that isn't that easy to understand.

Basically, what they're looking for here is, are you looking to find ways in the workplace to be more efficient and more effective? It doesn't have to be about big changes in your organisation. It could be just about things that you're doing. What are you doing to try and become more efficient and more effective? And remember, you can be really efficient at doing something completely ineffectively!

I'll let that settle in for a moment. You can be really efficient at doing something that's really ineffective. I'll give an example of that. You might be producing results, but are these the results of what people (your bosses) are looking for? So, if you're producing good results but it's not what people are looking for, it's not what the organisation's looking for, then what you're doing has merit (it's efficient) but it doesn't have value and worth (it isn't effective?).

So, think about that in your day-to-day tasks. What is it that you're doing that if you stop doing it, then it wouldn't make any difference? And what is it that you're doing now where if you increase your effectiveness, it will add more value to the organisation that you are a part of? Whether that be in the workplace or volunteering or in a sporting organisation. This is about you finding ways to work more efficiently and more effectively.

Like I said, you can be really efficient at doing something ineffective. So, we want to make sure that we are producing results that add value and worth. We want to increase our value in what we do and our worth in what we do, so that the organisation we work or volunteer for becomes more effective. Hopefully that makes sense for you? Again, this is something I go into in the online courses and in the interactive webinars to make sure people understand this concept and how to frame it in an interview answer. But you're not at that point just yet, at this moment in time you are just about gathering evidence for your application form. But how do we do this? We gather evidence of what we have done by recording it in a diary.

So every time you've had one of the experiences that demonstrates one or more of the behaviours in the Competency and Values Framework, you need to write about it in your diary using the following headings:

What happened?

What were you aiming to achieve?

What options did you consider?

What actions did you take? (Describe how you did things, not just what you did)

What was the result?

What could you have done better next time?

We're following a bit of a learning cycle there, so that when it comes to writing your application form and answering interview questions, you're not doing what a lot of people are doing, which is scratching their heads thinking, 'I can't think of an example!'

You are intentionally engineering opportunities for these things to happen; you're putting yourself in situations to develop your skills against the CVF behaviours. Once you've made a record of these situations in your diary you can look back on them and duplicate them in your application form or duplicate them in your interview answers. Straight away you're going to be awesome because you've worked towards the things that make the perfect police officer in the Competency and Values Framework.

So, I hope this makes sense to you folks. If it doesn't for any reason, then please feel free to ask me questions. Go to the Facebook Group and send me a personal message, or you could just email me at info@bluelightconsultancy.com. I'll be happy to go through any of this with you.

So, I hope you've enjoyed this challenging chapter. You might have to read it one or two times over. But the one thing that I'd say to you is just get stuck in, just start trying to do more of the behaviours required by the CVF and start trying to record them as evidence in your diary, in your daybook, whatever you choose to call it. I sometimes call it a 'Challenge Diary' because these are all challenges for you. These are all things where you'll be taking uncomfortable action, uncomfortable because for many of you, it'll be the first time you've done these things. For example, it might be the first time you've challenged someone's inappropriate behaviour.

Can I share something with you? About the first time I challenged someone's inappropriate behaviour? It didn't go that well and it was really, really hard to do. And I kind of messed it up because it ended up being a bit of an argument when it shouldn't have been an argument. And it didn't produce the results which I was hoping it was going to do.

So, it's not all going to go perfectly first-time, folks. But that's what they want to hear about in your interview. They don't want to hear about how everything you touch 'turns to gold' because that's not the reality of the world and they won't believe you. If you're describing in an interview a time when you dealt with something that was particularly challenging that you'd not experienced before, they're not expecting it to have gone perfectly.

The interviewers will want to hear how you've tried to do something and want to hear what the learning was because of it, what you'd do differently next time if you're faced with the same situation. Or if you could go back in time and experience the same thing again, what would you do differently? And it's not just about saying how for example, you'd ask better questions. Let's get specific here about the sort of questions that you would ask, or how you would listen to someone, how you'd go about demonstrating to the other person that you're listening.

https://bluelightonline.co.uk/book

Chapter 4 - 'Plugging In' - Developing your Police DNA!

In this chapter, I'm going to talk to you about 'plugging in.' What do I mean by that? Well, this is where you're going to work towards adopting the very 'DNA' of the force you want to join, and to make sure that you are aware of everything you need to know and understand about it before you join. Imagine you're like a stick of rock, and we cut you in half, the words 'police' will be written on the inside of it. So, you're going to obsess about police. You're going to obsess about the force that you want to join.

And the reason why we do this is so that by the time we get to the interview, we'll know more than the interviewer does about the force. So, if they're asking you questions about the current challenges, you're going to be able to speak eloquently about them and the things that you think you could do to contribute to meeting those challenges.

Similarly, with the application form, it's going to ask you questions about why you want to join this force. It's a popular question on the application form. So, you're going to have a really good working knowledge of the force, and you'll be able to speak eloquently and write eloquently about why you want to join that force.

So, 'pin your ears back,' folks. We are now going to go through so many things that I'd like you to look up. A lot of these things you won't know about, because you don't know what you don't know. But the good thing is, I know the things that you need to know about. And so that's what I'm going to do in this chapter. I'm going to share with you all the things you need to do to make sure that you are living and breathing the force that you want to join and living and breathing police. This is how obsessive you need to be. Those clients of mine who are successful in everything first time. They're the ones who obsess like the obsessiveness I'm going to talk about in this chapter.

The first thing we need to do is we need to become familiar with the actual makeup of the force. You'll be able to find out all this information in the force website: the makeup of the force in terms of its size; its geography; who the senior leaders are; who the chief officers are; how it's broken up into divisions or boroughs, and what specialist units exist. So, all that information should be available on their website.

It's also, I think, interesting just to find out a little bit about the history of the force, and that won't be hard to find out, you just need to Google it. Google 'history' and then the name of the police force that you want to join and there'll be people who have written up things of interest. There'll be articles in there I'm quite sure, troll through it. This isn't necessarily really important, but it's always good to have a little bit of background information.

Now, we're going to get into the nuts and bolts of what the force is about. So, we want to take a look at the priorities, and where are we going to find that out? Well, use Google again, but this timer for the Strategic Plan for the force that you want to join. Every force must have a Strategic Plan. It might be published on the Policing and Crime Commissioner's website. So, take a look at who the Policing and Crime Commissioner is and what they're about.

If you're joining a force like the Metropolitan Police or Greater Manchester Police, they won't have a Policing and Crime Commissioner, they will have a mayor, they'll also have the mayor's office for policing. In London, that's MOPAC, the Mayor's Office for Policing and Crime in London, and they will have so much information on their websites that's really, useful background information for you.

So from there, once we've read the Strategic Plan, and we've got a good feel about the direction the force is going in, the challenges, what's going well, and what the chief officers are saying about it. We're now going to take a look at the values of the force. Now, the values for the force aren't necessarily going to be just a repeat of what's in The Competency and Values Framework and in The Code of Ethics, although it might be. However, some forces like Northumbria have their own very individual and unique values, and they will assess you against those unique and individual values as well as against the CVF.

So, now is the time to start becoming familiar with what they are and start thinking in terms of those values, as in what parts of those values do I need to develop myself against? I know I'm crossing over into the chapter where we've already discussed how to develop yourself against the Competency and Values Framework, but this is something more I'd like you to do. Start thinking about the values of the force, and then start thinking, 'well, where am I on the scale of decision-making?' As in an example value, 'that our officers will make the right decisions at the right time with the right partners and for the right reasons.' That sort of thing. Those are the values you will see. So, what's your decision-making like? Are you a strong decision-maker? Or do you need to flex those decision-making muscles and develop them a little bit more?

From there, we're going to take a look at Her majesty's Inspectorate of Constabulary, actually, it's, Her Majesty's Inspectorate of Constabulary, Fire & Rescue Services, HMICFRS, that's a long abbreviation. That's two inspectorates that were brought together under one umbrella, but the part that you're interested in is the Her Majesty's Inspectorate of Constabulary. Every force is inspected by HMIC and the HMIC reports are publicly available - they will tell you what's going well in the force and what they need to start focusing on more. For those things that are going well, read upon them and find out more about those things. But equally, the things that are challenges, read up on those as well and start thinking, 'when I'm in this police force, what can I do to contribute to enabling the force to meet these challenges that have been set for them by HMIC?'

From here, we're going to look at social media, and of course, it goes without saying that you're going to follow all the Bluelight (my!) accounts. If you go to the 'Offer Wall' at the end of this chapter, you'll find links to all those accounts. The reason why I'd like you to do that is because every day, I put out new information which is going to be useful for you.

Also, take a look at the YouTube account for the force that you're joining, and make sure you subscribe to that. Some forces have awesome YouTube channels, and they're always putting out information about latest operations or some challenges they're facing. Forces like Leicestershire Constabulary even have videos from Simon Cole, their Chief Constable. He actually publishes a vlog where he talks to the camera, which I think is just awesome.

From there, move on to Facebook. Look at the force's Facebook account. Make sure that you follow that page and any Facebook accounts for neighbourhood policing teams or any specialist units. Make sure you follow those and troll through them on a regular basis. And by the way, this is like 30 minutes a day minimum on social media. Forget all those other social media accounts you follow. You're going to obsess about the police now.

Twitter is an awesome source of information. Take a look at my account and see who I am following and who I'm retweeting. Look at the accounts of the chief officers for the force you want to join and then pay attention to who they are following, because this is where you're going to find out information about all the things that are going on locally, and all the things they are involved with as well. There are loads of useful information on Twitter and it's a good way of connecting and seeing how their police connect with other organisations as well.

Similarly for Instagram, probably mostly pictures if they've got an Instagram account at all. Then there is LinkedIn. The force might not have a LinkedIn account, but what they will have is lots of individuals from that force who have LinkedIn accounts. Look to follow them and link in with them, because they often publish information about the latest challenges, the latest initiatives, the latest operations, mostly things that are going well, but a great read. A great way to get lots of information about the force that you want to join.

And if you manage to connect with individuals there, there's no problem with just firing off a quick message at them. Once you've liked or commented on a few of their posts you can then fire across a little message to say, 'is there any chance I could have a 5-minute chat with you about being a police officer in your force?'

This is how you're going to build up connections, and this is how you're going to find out a little bit more about the force from the people who work in it. Forces like British Transport Police give you extra marks in your interview if you have gone out of your way to discover more about the force by visiting a police station or speaking to serving police officers.

Right. I hope you're still with me. There's more to come, a lot more to come.

So, I'd like you to also look for the news on your force and those individuals who are in your force. And the way we're going to do that is we're going to set up something called Google Alerts. Now, you might not have known that Google Alerts exist, but it does. You need a Google account, a Gmail account, and from there, you're just going to google Google Alerts and it'll tell you how to set up Google Alerts. I use them every day. I've got about a hundred alerts set up for phrases like 'police recruitment,' 'asset-based community development,' 'neighbourhood policing,' the names of several chief constables, and a lot more.

Once you have set up Google Alerts, it means that every time anything is published, anywhere in the world actually, on that subject, or that name, or that location, it will send you an email automatically to say that this phrase has appeared in this news article or in this YouTube video, or whatever it might be. Google is constantly trolling the net, looking for those phrases on your behalf, and it's free, which means it's an awesome service. You get to find out about the force, and the news is brought to you using Google Alerts. Please do use this service, I think it's absolutely fantastic.

Now, we want to find out a little bit more about which partners the force works with. So not just the council, the fire service, and the health service, but housing associations, mental health teams, and social services. Look at the Community Safety Partnerships (CSPs) that exist within the force area that you are going to apply to. You'll find that every CSP will also have a plan, some are really good and others, not as extensive as they should be. I've seen some that are quite poor, but I've seen the others that are really awesome and very, very detailed in terms of what they're trying to achieve. Every police force must have a Community Safety Partnership. This was set in stone by law in the Crime and Disorder Act of 1998, which basically required organisations, which have a responsibility for crime and safety, and the welfare of a community, to work together to ensure that they are doing everything they can to prevent harm coming to their community and to bring offenders to justice.

Once offenders are brought to justice, how are they going to be managed? So, take a look at the probation service, what is it they do? Find out what happens to offenders once they go to prison and once they get released. A lot of reading there for you to do and a lot of research for you to do, but it will pay off. I absolutely promise you it'll pay off.

So, from here, we should be starting to work out now what the challenges are for the force that you want to apply to join. And this is extremely relevant because you could be asked this question either on your application form or at your interview. And it might just be as open as, 'tell me about the challenges this force is facing?' And the next question you could be asked is, 'if you were to be successful in the application process, how would you help us meet those challenges?' And that's why it's important to have all this background research in your head, in your DNA, so that you can just 'plug into' the force. You shouldn't start on day one thinking, so who's the chief constable? Strategic? I've never heard of the strategic plan! You're the one that's going to know more than the trainers, I promise you. I absolutely promise you; you'll know more than the trainers.

Okay. You might be thinking that's the end of this chapter. No, it's not, because this is just the police on a local level. I'd like you to also become really interested in what's going on in policing at a national level. So, look at the work of the National Crime Agency and look at the work the Border Force does as well. Two national organisations that very much link into the work the police are doing locally.

Also, look at the National Police Chiefs Council and the strategic plans they have. Find out who in your chief officer team is the lead for different elements of policing within the National Police Chief's Council. Some of the more senior chief constables will have responsibility for things like firearms and organised criminality. The lower down the pecking order you get as a chief officer, you might have something like responsibility for something like dog bites or something not quite as important, important if you're bitten by a dog, of course, but not quite as important or high up on the pecking order as things like organised crime and firearms.

Also, the National Police Chief's Council have got a vision for the future for policing. So, that's something else you can talk about in your interview.

Now, there's also other organisations out there which link into policing like the Police Foundation. It's well worth linking in with the Police Foundation and getting newsletters from them, which you can get free of charge. Just go to their website, where you can sign you up and subscribe to their newsletters. Lots of online conferences and lots of publications on things like the future challenges for the police and what is the role of the police? A lot of really interesting things come out in the Police Foundation. I've spoken at two of their conferences in the past. They're a great bunch of individuals who are very, very dedicated to doing what they can to help support the police.

Also, subscribe to magazines like Police Professional.

Now, at this point in the chapter, you might be thinking, 'stop Brendan. That's enough!'

But no, I'm still not finished. So, I want you to also get really interested in some of the associated issues that the police are facing. Things like complexity in terms of a public health approach to policing. Take a look at the work of the Violence Reduction Units that are dotted around the country. Most of them are based on the work of the Scottish Violent Reduction Unit. Scotland was the first country in Europe that decided it was going to take violent crime and not treat it as a crime problem, but to treat it as a public health problem. This is where we get that phrase, 'A public health approach to policing.' I think it probably would have been worded better if it was called, 'a community welfare and existence approach to policing,' which would have linked in nicely with the Peelian Principles.

You don't know what the Peelian Principles are? That is something else to look up. Look up the Peelian Principles, which were set in stone in 1829. Sir Robert Peel, the founder of the modern-day police service, the founder of the Metropolitan Police, established those principles as guidance for police officers in 1829 to follow. They are as good today as they were back then. Actually, they're probably more important today than they were back then. I used to have a copy of them on the wall in my office next to my desk. That's how important I thought they were.

Also, look at issues that link in with Violence Reduction Units, such as the causes of crime and the causes of lots of complex social problems. I'd like you also to do some research and read up on Adverse Childhood Experiences, where you'll be able to see the links between, not just the police, but also other partner organisations and other complex social problems as the drivers of crime, and the drivers of all sorts of other behaviours and problems that exist within this wider social context.

What you're going to find is how many social issues are incredibly complex, but that's what policing is today, and we need to start preparing you now for that complex world.

I can share with you that the world I joined in 1985 of policing was a lot simpler than it is today. Today, it is highly, highly complex, and it's only by understanding all the different threads that I've just mentioned that you're going to really getting a feel for what the role of the police officer is. You're going to discover that it's not just arresting people, although, that is a really important part of your role. It is far more multiple-dimensional than that.

So, please do read up on all those things that I've talked about in this chapter. It will serve you really well.

https://bluelightonline.co.uk/book

Chapter 5 - Overview of the Police Recruitment Process

In this chapter, we're going to look at over 50 varieties of how to get into the police, an overview of what comes after the application form. I say over 50 varieties because in there are over 50 police forces in that make up the constabularies of the United Kingdom. They include the 43 Home Office forces of England and Wales, Police Scotland, Police Service of Northern Ireland, Isle of Man Police, Channel Islands Police forces, Ports Police, Civil Nuclear Constabulary, British Transport Police, and the Ministry of Defence Police.

With so many forces there are also over 50 different approaches to getting in and a lot of those approaches can just change overnight. For example, Derbyshire Constabulary, at the time of writing, have just changed the nature of their In-Force interview. It still involves a presentation, but they have changed the title of the presentation. It still involves a task for you to carry out, but that's changed as well. So, everything changes. The only thing that stays fairly consistent, for those of you who are applying to Home Office forces and to the Civil Nuclear Constabulary, who also use it at this moment in time, is the College of Policing Online Assessment Centre. However, post COVID, that is also likely to change (The Metropolitan Police are currently developing a new assessment process).

So, what do forces do to make everything so different? Well, every Force involves an application form. That's where they screen out, sometimes thousands of people, because they can only actually cope with a certain number for their own online assessment, the College of Policing assessment centres, and In-force / Final interviews. Your application form must be an amazing success to ensure you get through to the next stage. Remember, the only purpose of an application form is to get you to whatever the next stage is.

HOW TO SUCCEED IN THE POLICE RECRUITMENT PROCESS

A typical recruitment process after your application looks like this. You'll be invited to the online assessment centre or the new version of the assessment centre, which is designed and run by the College of Policing. The reason why there is a National Assessment Centre is because, when I joined in 1985, every force had their own version, unique versions, of a recruitment process. There was absolutely no standardisation and apart from the current National Assessment Centre, there still isn't.

So, you do the In Force Online Assessments and with my guidance, you pass them. This will be followed by The College of Policing Assessment Centre, same deal, follow my guidance and pass that. Then typically, you'll have a force interview or, if it's The Metropolitan Police (at the time of writing), it's onto role plays. If you are going for The Metropolitan Police using the degree holder, direct entry detective route, then you will need to do an in-tray and a briefing exercise in front of a detective sergeant or detective inspector.

But it's not just the Metropolitan Police who are different. If you're going for North Yorkshire Police, it is an interview, but they call it strength-based interview. Other forces, such as Derbyshire, have a presentation. A lot of forces will ask you questions along the lines of, 'Can you tell me about a time when....?' Other forces might ask you those types of questions and questions, like, 'How would you manage this type of situation.......?' or, 'How would you go about doing community engagement?'

You might be asked questions about your values. You might be asked questions about your contribution to the force. 'What sort of contribution are you going to be able to make?' And here's a tough motivation question, 'Why you? Why now?'

You could have situational questions, where they give you a certain situation, and they want a really detailed breakdown of how you're going to deal with it. They could also give you problem-solving exercises. One force gives you the task to go find a local problem and describe how you would deal with it as a police officer.

As you can see from this, it's not just a force interview. Different forces call them different things. So, some of them will call them a final interview. Some of them will call them an in-force interview. Some of them will call them an in-force presentation. Some of them, Essex, and Kent call them senior interviews, as you will be interviewed by a senior officer.

Just to confuse things even more, some forces will do all the in-force assessment before the College of Policing National Assessment Centre. Confused? If you are, don't worry. The chapters that come after this are going to be able to help you work out what each one of these stages involves.

This is just a short overview to give you a flavour for what you need to do to start preparing, because all those forces I've described that use all those techniques, they could change them all tomorrow. So many forces have done this. They'll try one thing for six months, and then they'll try something else for six months, and then they'll settle on something for a year or two. Then some new boss comes in and decides, 'actually, I don't like that.' So, they'll change everything again. Change is the only consistent thing in the police, so, get over it and get used to it.

Once you've got through all of assessment and interviews, the next stage typically involves a fitness test. Now is when you should be starting to prepare for the fitness test. Don't think just because you can run a mile in a decent time that you be able to manage the fitness test because the fitness test isn't just about being able to run to 5.4 on the bleep test. It's being able to follow the rules of the bleep test to the letter. Quite a few of my clients have failed in the past, really fit people, because they've not followed the instructions. If you do not follow instructions during the fitness test, you'll be given a warning, if you fail to do something about that warning, then you're pulled out. That's it – you've failed.

Go to the webinars that are part of the 'Offer Wall' in this book (at the end of every chapter). This is where you will find a guidance video on how to make sure that you smash the bleep test. Start preparing for it now because while you can start last minute preparation for an interview with a few days' notice (although far from ideal), one of the things that you can't do with a few days' notice is get your fitness in order. The same goes for the other aspects of the pre-employment checks, such as vetting. So, make sure that your referees, the people who you're going to be using as references, know that they're going to get a letter or an email from your constabulary that you're applying to. Make sure that you've got everything in order in terms of any associations. So, if you have an association in the family, for example, that has a criminal background, you need to be able to explain it in a huge amount of detail. More about vetting in other chapters.

You'll also have a medical to prepare for. So, make sure that you've dug out, from the force that you are applying to, all their medical requirements. Why now? Because so many of my clients, get through every part of the recruitment process except this. They're so pleased, they're so proud to have achieved so much, and then they fail at the medical. They might have failed the medical on something that might be a long-term issue. They could have saved themselves a lot of heartache because they would have discovered how with their medical condition, they could never be a police officer. Although you may think it's unfair, a lot of those medical pre-requirements are there to ensure that you'd be able to manage the physical demands of the service.

They're also going to check on your educational qualifications towards the end of the process. So, make sure that your educational qualifications meet the requirements of the constabulary that you're applying to. Again, as there's fifty-something different varieties of how to get into the police, there's fifty-something different requirements of what they want from you.

In terms of educational qualifications (at the time of writing), Merseyside police just want two GCSEs in Maths and English. By the way, if you're going to do the Police Constable Degree Apprenticeship, it's a government condition of the funding for the apprenticeship that you must have a GCSE in Maths and English. So, it's not down to the force. What is down to the force is anything on top of that.

So, Merseyside have decided, 'that's the minimum. So that's all we're going to require.' I spoke to Andy Cook, the previous Chief Constable, about this, and his views were very clear that, 'Well if that's the only requirement, that's all I want. I don't want to preclude people have got life experience.' Serena Kennedy, who's the new Chief Constable at Merseyside Police, seems to have taken the same sort of view. She was the deputy alongside Andy Cook previously, and she's followed the same process, just wants two GCSEs.

Serena was a probationer on my team when I was a sergeant in G.M.P. She's done really well. Well done, Serena. And well-done Andy Cook on your 'retirement' (he's gone onto a very senior position in Her Majesty's Inspectorate of Constabulary). I joined with Andy and he's the last one standing out of my intake. A bit of useless information for you there!

So, what else can I tell you about Qualifications? Make sure you've got the certificates. So, if you can't find the certificates now, don't wait until a couple of days before you get the email that says, 'please can you present us with the originals of your educational qualifications.' The time to start digging them out of the attic is now. The time to discover you've not got them anymore is now, so you can apply for replacements to the awarding body. That might require you to get in touch with your school and college to find out who the awarding body was.

Make sure you put the right grades down as well, because so many of my clients have come back to me to say, 'hey, I thought I got a B. I didn't. I just got a D. What do I do?" Well, you've just got to 'fess up.' Therefore, it's important that you are ticking off every one of the boxes all the way through the recruitment program. That's what this book is for. It's to help you tick off those boxes. So, you're in good company.

There you go, folks. That, in a nutshell, is the process. Once you've got through all of that, then you will get a conditional offer. Bear in mind that most recruitment teams are understaffed, under-resourced, and sometimes under-experienced. You may have to chase them up, follow them up, and may have to explain things to them as well. Just today, one of my clients has got back in touch me to say he's had a job offer from a particular constabulary for a start date that's three weeks away. You see the problem with that? Most employers want you to give them a month's notice, so he can't join in three weeks' time.

So, that's a force that does not plan things out very well. You'll find a lot of that going on. It seems to be endemic within the service. My own personal view is the whole recruitment process needs a good shakeup. It's not that different to the one I went through in 1985 in that it's very linear. You might be thinking, 'why does it take a year and a half to two years for some forces to get me from when I apply to a warrant card in my pocket?' The reason is because everything is done in a linear process. First the application form, then comes the online assessment centre, then comes the interview then comes your fitness, then comes all the pre-employment checks and vetting. I do not know one force that does them all at the same time. You might be thinking, 'well, that would make incredible sense, wouldn't it?' It would, but it'd also be quite expensive because vetting is an expensive process. Medical, an expensive process. Running the fitness tests, an expensive process. All the way through this, they are whittling the numbers down and trying to keep the expenses down.

When I say the word whittling the numbers down, in some forces, it can be just 1 in 25 that get to the end of the recruitment process. So, just 1 in 25 gets in. In other forces, it's better than that, it's about 1 in 8. It varies depending on supply and demand.

There are other circumstances that could get in the way of your application success - some forces will tell you that you've passed everything, but you'll then get one of those emails that says, 'Unfortunately, on this occasion, the next intakes are full and as your overall marks were not high enough, we will be terminating your application. However, we may have a vacancy for you in the future.'

So, you're left in a kind of limbo. You might be thinking, 'What do I do there?' Well, at the time of writing, the College of Policing rules are that you can apply to as many police forces you want, but you can only set the assessment centre once in any 6-month period. So, apply to as many forces as you can.

I do know of officers who have gone back to do the assessment centre with a different force, having achieved a result that wasn't high enough to get through to the next stage. They waited six months and then have gone back to do it again to get a higher mark. They do this so they can go back into the pool for that force or into a pool for another force and guarantee that they're going to get through to the next stage.

Others have simply got that email, and they've had to wait it out because of their family situation or other circumstances. They can't move to different force area. So, they've had to wait it out. For some individuals, that's not worked out well because they've had to wait for two or three years. Surrey did this quite a few years ago. They made people wait for about three years and then just wrote to them to say, 'actually, we don't have a place for any of you. Your vetting, new medical and fitness.... everything's run out now. But Sussex are recruiting now, why don't you try them?'

Humberside Police kept people in a recruitment pool for about two years, promising them how at some point, you'll get some news on an intake date. Some people waited up to two years, which I think is completely unacceptable. But it doesn't matter what you or I think. Remember the 'Golden Rule,' how those who hold the gold make the rules. So, the force recruitment teams, the College of Policing, they hold the gold, they make the rules. All we've got to do, folks, is make sure we comply with them. Comply with every requirement that they make so that you are going to be successful.

That's why I will keep pushing you in the chapters that follow this. I'll keep talking to you about achieving the highest mark possible. We are not just after a pass because simply getting a pass with many forces is not going to get you through to the next stage. They can pick and choose candidates. You might be thinking, 'well, that sounds so unfair?' But remember, they don't owe you a living, and none of this is going to be given to you on a silver platter. There's no magic bullet. You've got to work hard at this, folks - it's always been that way. When I joined in 1985 and, apologies if the sounds like a 'salty old sea dog story,' but there was a total of about six day's worth of assessments – three days and two nights of that was in the Welsh mountains being absolutely 'beasted' through all sorts of weird and wonderful exercises. Only 1 in 40 applicants got into the Cheshire Constabulary in 1985.

It's always been a difficult profession to get into, but because you've got the best company ever, in the form of me, to guide you through the process, we can reduce those odds.

But it's only going to happen if you work hard. So, I know you might be sick of me saying this, but remember, you've got to work hard. You've got to take that action on a daily basis. You've got to recognise that your actions are imperfect at times because it's not always going to work out how you want it to work out. Your sample interview question, the practice that you do, it's all about building up that culture of momentum, so the action you take daily keeps improving you all the way to the point where you are coming across prepared and confident at every stage. Prepared and confident as opposed to being rehearsed and dithery or not knowing what you're doing or not knowing how to answer the questions in the interview.

There's nothing worse than that. So, I know I'm going to keep repeating this, but it needs to be like a mission within you that you take that imperfect action daily. That will serve you well to get the high marks you will deserve.

https://bluelightonline.co.uk/book

Chapter 6 - The Application Form

Now, the title of this chapter is all about application form questions. So, if you have got an idea of the sort of questions that you are going to be asked, prior to receiving an application form, then you are in a really good position to start preparing yourself so that you have got the evidence to write about and submit. This really is something to focus on as so many of my clients I have supported over the years have struggled with this.

Most of my clients have always had the desire to join the police but instead of being pro-active in preparing for the application stage. They've just plodded along through their life, they do their job, have some hobbies, do some sports, get involved in activities, and then they decide they are going to apply to join the police, but just continue to plod along with their lives and not do anything extraordinary to move closer to their goal of becoming a police officer.

That process starts now, it starts today for you.

It does not start tomorrow, nor does it start next week. It starts today, and the reason why it is going to start today is because I am going to give you the typical questions that are asked on the application forms, which means you can start preparing for them. I'll show you how to do that also.

Now, you might be thinking that all application forms are going to be the same - no they are not. Several years ago, just about every police force used the National Competency-Based application form the College of Policing provided. However, the problem with this is that they are marked against something called the Policing Professional Framework.

Now, the Policing Professional Framework and the competency system that came with it went out of the window in 2016 (if my memory serves me well) and was replaced by the Competency and Values Framework. However, the College of Policing did not provide a replacement application form to account for the Competency and Values Framework.

So a lot of forces still do use this old framework, this old application form, and that is what I am going to go through first with you. I'm going to tell you what all the questions are. However, several forces now use their own unique questions. This is becoming more in vogue now, I'm seeing more and more Forces ask fewer questions, but they want a bigger word count, so they want a lot more detail from you.

So, what I am going to do first, I am going to go through the National Application Form questions because the force you go for may still choose to use those, and then I am going to give you some examples from other forces which have gone their own way.

So, pin your ears back folks, this is the National Application Form which is still used. It is old, it should have been discarded a long time ago, but you know the 'Golden Rule' applies. Those who hold the gold make the rules. I do not make the rules because I do not hold the gold!

So the first question is professionalism. All these questions, by the way, are broken down into sub-questions, so:

Question 1: Professionalism

Please describe a specific occasion when you have intervened to take control of a situation.

The sub-questions:

Why was it necessary to intervene in the situation?

What did you do to take control of the situation?

What did you consider when intervening in the situation?

What was particularly good or effective about how you intervened to take control of the situation?

What difficulties did you experience and how did you overcome them?

Question 2: Working with others.

Please describe a specific occasion when you have encouraged a person to view an issue more positively.

Sub-questions:

Why was it necessary to encourage the person to view the issue more positively?

How did you encourage the person to view the issue more positively?

What did you consider when encouraging the person to view the issue more positively?

What was particularly good or effective about how you encourage the person to view the issue more positively?

What difficulties did you experience and how did you overcome them?

Question 3: Decision making

Please describe a specific occasion when you have considered a number of options before making a decision.

Why was it necessary to consider a number of options before making the decision?

What did you consider when identifying the options?

What did you consider when making the decision?

What was particularly good or effective about you, how did you identify the options and made the decision?

What difficulties did you experience? And how did you overcome them?

Question 4: Service delivery

Please describe a specific occasion when you have had to manage your time effectively in order to complete a task.

Why did you have to manage your time effectively in order to complete the task?

How did you manage your time effectively in order to complete the task?

What did you consider to make sure you completed the task?

What was particularly good or effective about how you manage your time?

What difficulties did you experience and how did you overcome them?

That's all the competency questions, the form then moves on to the next part, which is about your motivation.

In questions 5 to 10 below, we want to know something about your motivations to be a police officer, we want to know your expectations of police work, and what preparation you have undertaken before applying.

These questions are important, and you may not progress to the next stage if you do not answer these questions fully. So do not make the mistake a lot of people make folks, which is thinking that these questions are not actually marked because they are, I know they are.

Question 5: Tell us why you want to become a police officer?

Question 6: Tell us why you have applied to your chosen Force?

Question 7: Tell us in some detail, what tasks you expect to be undertaking as a police officer?

Question 8: Tell us what effect, you expect being a police officer to have on your social and domestic life?

Question 9: What preparation have you undertaken before making this application to ensure that you know what to expect and that you are prepared for the role of a police officer?

Question 10: If you previously applied to be a police officer, Special Constable or Police Community Support Officer, what have you done since your last application to better prepare yourself for the role of a Police Officer?

Now, folks, that is it, that is the end of the application form. You have got quite a tight word count on this application form, most of most forces only give you something like 80 words per question and per sub-question.

However, I have seen some forces give you 600 or 700 characters and some people have misread it, 'I thought it meant words,' and they have completed a massive application form, which would fail straight away because you have gone way beyond the word count. So read the form really carefully, what the word count is, and what the character count is if they are doing it that way. Now, some of you might be thinking where is the advice on how to answer those questions? That is coming in the next chapter, do not worry about that, it will be in the next chapter.

In the next chapter I am going to go through common mistakes that people make, and how to avoid them. I think that is the best way of outlining how to approach those sorts of questions.

Now, when it comes to other forces, I told you how some forces are now doing their own thing, so I'll give you some examples from Greater Manchester Police. They only ask two questions, but they want a 500-word answer.

Question 1: Why do you want to join the police and why Greater Manchester Police? How do you think your skills, experience, and knowledge link to this role?

500 Words.

Question 2: What have you done to benefit the communities where you live?

500 Words

They used to say, of Greater Manchester but they have stopped that now because it stumped people who applied from outside of Greater Manchester.

So, this is looking at the levels of citizenship which you have demonstrated, so start doing things that demonstrate citizenship.

Update prior to publication – GMP have just changed this question to:

Tell us about a time when you have had to adapt your skills to meet the needs and requirements of different groups or communities and any challenges you faced

500 Words.

The question could return to the previous one!

Now, let's take a look at another Force, Lincolnshire Police. They have a direct entry detective programme - they ask a layer of questions on top of the old-style application form that I have just gone through.

The additional questions they ask you:

They want you to explain in 750 words:

How do you meet these following skills: problem-solving; communication skills; IT skills; the ability to work as part of a team or with partners; the ability to build an effective working relationship; and (for the detective pathway) experience in an investigatory role.

The latter is only a desirable trait in case you have not had that kind of experience.

So that is an example of an add-on.

Here is an example of a force that is making it clear that you are being assessed against the Competency and Values Framework, and that is Lancashire Constabulary. Here you have three questions:

Question 1: The competency of being emotionally aware

In no more than 500 words, provide evidence of your ability to effectively engage with minority groups or communities within Lancashire and give some examples.

You might want to include sort of the challenges that is minority groups face.

How you have worked or interacted with minority groups?

How you have communicated in other languages and any other relevant skills experience or learning.

500 words.

Question 2: The competency of Deliver, Support and Inspire.

In no more than 300 words. Please provide an example of where you have overcome challenges in order to achieve a personal or professional priority.

Question 3: The competency of Analyse Critically

In no more than 300 words, provide an example of where you have analysed information in order to make a decision or recommendation, including the options, the benefits, and the risks you considered.

So you can see above how a few forces have deliberately taken responsibility there with Lancashire, Greater Manchester Police, and Lincolnshire police and how they have created their own application form. The one for Lancashire I think is particularly challenging because if you have not set your stall out, to effectively engage and learn about minority groups and get involved with working alongside minority groups in some shape or form, then you are not going to be able to answer that first question.

Similarly, if you do not push yourself in the workplace or in the volunteering that you do or in a part-time job or in a sport that you are part of, you'll struggle with the second Deliver, Support and inspire questions. When I say push yourself, I do not mean running faster, I mean, push yourself and challenge your skills, and in respect of how you interact with the rest of the organisation you are part of.

The 3rd one, analyse critically. So, this wants to know about your decision-making skills - unless you are flexing your decision-making skills on a regular basis you will also struggle. I am not talking about just following a process here and I am not talking about big decisions in your life like where you go to university, or what job you are going to apply for, or marriage breakups. I have had one client who tried to persuade me that his marriage breakup was a big decision. No, these are life decisions, they're different.

What they are looking for is times when you have put yourself in situations where you have had to make difficult decisions and you had to consider all the different options, the benefits, and the risks in order to make that decision. So, by going through that process, the decision becomes less difficult and easier to make.

There you go folks, as more challenging questions crop up from different forces, I will, of course, update you. They won't be in this book though - the updates will be in the Police Application Form Blueprint, which is a short course / programme I put together for people who are applying to join the police service. They also have their own dedicated Facebook group, where I can update the clients of that group and give them access to the latest guidance and advice.

For the future, I anticipate more forces using very, very challenging questions, similar to what Lancashire uses and very similar to what the Greater Manchester Police do as well. So it is worth you keeping on top of all the different variations and continually thinking about, 'right, so now is the time I start collecting evidence for……, now is the time I start preparing myself for……., now is the time I start pushing myself and challenging myself to do……'

As I said earlier in this chapter, doing what most people do by just waiting for the application form to come out and then to look back in time and think, 'I am struggling for examples,' is not where you want to be.

Many my clients tell me how they are struggling to think of times when they have done certain things asked for. Well, if they knew that they were going to be asked about those certain things 12 months before, they could have started to get prepared for it. That is what I am doing with you here, making sure that you are prepared for that process.

So, this chapter has been quite factual so far, but one that is necessary is to give you a flavour for how your initial assessment is going to be conducted. This will be your first contact with the police force that you are applying to, and it is so important to get it right folks. Which is why the next chapter, where I go through the common mistakes that I have seen being made over the decade that I have been marking and assessing client's application forms, will be so helpful for you.

It is so important that you get the application form right in other ways also, because this is the only stage where they can screen a big percentage of candidates out.

Some forces open the recruitment window for a short period of time, as Cheshire did just recently. They opened on a Monday, when one of my clients applied for an application form that afternoon. It was only the Monday afternoon of the first day and they had an application form with the number 2500 and something on it. So already they had had over two and a half thousand people asking for application forms. What happened next? On the Wednesday morning they closed the window. So the window was only open for such a short time, once they got to a certain point where they couldn't cope with any more application forms coming in, they closed the window.

My client had an application form pre-prepared so that as soon as she got the application form, all she had to do is just cut and paste the answers into the spaces and then get the application form submitted before they closed the window. I estimated they probably had about 4,000 applications and they needed to screen that down to something like 1,000, which is a manageable number.

So that's 3/4 of the applicants that are going to get screened out at the application form stage, and depending on how many people they have got applying and how many application forms have got accepted, they can either up the marks or lower the marks, depending on how many people they need and how many people they have got who are capable of actually doing all the interviews, the online assessment centres and all the marking that goes with it. They do not have unlimited resources to do all those things.

Durham Constabulary used to mark people on each answer with an A to a D, where any answer with a D was an automatic failure. Eventually, they got to the point where you had to have an A in every answer to go through to the next stage and people who had B's in some of their answers were put into what was like a 'holding bay' just in case they needed anyone else to come forward because sufficient people did not pass the next stages.

So that is how competitive it is folks, and that is why you should focus so much on getting through this next stage because remember, the only point of an application form is to get you to the next stage of the process, to get to the assessment centre or to get you to interview. It serves no other purpose. Once you have got through the application form stage, no one is going to look at your application form again.

If the force is still at the point after they have done the application form screening, they have done the interview screening, they have done the online assessment centre screening and they still have too many candidates, they may have to turn people away still. As an example, a force may have recruited for an intake of 25 individuals, and another intake 6 months later for another 25 individuals, which is a total of 50. If they have got 80 people who have got through every stage, they need to have some form of criteria to select the 50 out of the 80. What they might do, many forces do this, is they will combine your score from your application form, your assessment centre, and your in-force interview, and they will rank people that way.

So, you may find yourself in a situation where you have passed everything, but you get an email to say, 'unfortunately, on this occasion, we do not have a position for you.' They will just put you in a 'holding bay,' and this holding bay can last for years. So, my advice here, if you can, is to try and find another force that will entertain your application. Remember, you can apply to as many police forces as you want.

Some forces still stick to their own, 'no, you can only apply to us you can not apply to any other forces' rule. In which case, get the link from the College of Policing website (if you cannot find it, ask me for it I will find it for you, just message me) and then show your force that guidance from the College of Policing. They do not have to follow it, by the way, it is only guidance, there is no law that says they have got to follow it, it is just good practice that they do.

But like I said, a lot of forces do not like you applying to other forces at the same time.

So, it is a complex process, folks. Make sure that you get every step in the application form phase right and then you will earn the right to go through to the next stage.

https://bluelightonline.co.uk/book

Chapter 7 - Common Application Form Mistakes and How to Avoid Them

In this chapter, what we're going to look at is the common application form mistakes. I think this is probably one of the best ways of advising you on how to complete your application form, by demonstrating some of the big mistakes, some of the shockers that people make on a regular basis. I've just taken these mistakes from two application forms that have been marked just recently.

One of the services I provide is to check your application form to make sure it's good to go. The initial submissions of both these application forms were horrible! They would never have got anywhere near the next stage. So, both individuals would have got this very nice email to say, 'Thank you very much for your interest in XXXX force. Unfortunately, on this occasion, your application form did not reach the required standard.'

Time to open your eyes folks. Here are 10... I might even elaborate, and it might turn into more than 10, common application form mistakes. Although these are just from two recent application forms, the issues I highlight are endemic in all the application forms that I've seen over the past 10 years or so.

1. Answer the Question!!

The very first mistake is people not actually answering the question. This is so important, for you to read the question that you're being asked and actually answer that question. Not the question you were hoping to be asked and not what you are trying to translate what they mean by that question into something completely different.

I'll give you an example here. This is an example where in the application form it asked about a time when you've encouraged someone to view a situation positively. What they did is they gave an example of when, in their role as a teaching assistant, they gave feedback to some parents about their child. The feedback was being discussed in the answer, at no point did this individual say that the parents didn't view the situation positively and why they didn't view it positively. However, it was a really good answer for the question, 'please can you tell me what about a time when you've given someone feedback about a situation?' Although the content was okay, it was the answer to a completely different question.

Make sure that you answer the question!

2. Be precise – vague won't cut it!

A lot of questions on application forms will say things like, 'What did you consider when you created options for making the decision?' I think this throws people and they tend to go into a very vague answers where they say things like, 'I considered my thoughts and my feelings. I considered what I was worried about.' No, just no! They don't want all those vague comments. What they're looking for is, what did you consider as in what would be the impact if you didn't do anything? What options did you consider? What pros and cons went with each one of those options? What sort of contingencies did you consider? Should you go down a certain path? That's the sort of thing they're looking at, not your feelings and your thoughts such as, 'I considered that I was really emotional at the time.' It's just so vague and it's just not answering the question and you're wasting your word count.

3. Less of the 'What,' more of the 'How!'

Candidates often make too many bold claims in their answers. When you're describing what you did, saying things like, 'I was calm and professional…. I approached the person and offered them empathy…. I reassured them…. I was positive in my communication…. I solved the problem…. I reassured them…. I used de-escalation techniques.'

Now, all these things sound great. They are a useful starting point for going into the next part that describes how you actually did those things. You've got to describe how you did something. There's no point in just making a bold claim that you, 'approached the person calmly and professionally' until you actually explain how you've done it.

Don't think you can follow the advice from elsewhere and just use buzzwords from the Competency and Values Framework. Saying things like, 'I collaborated with my fellow team members in an organisationally beneficial way. Focusing on producing an effective and efficient answer to the problem that we were facing.' Sounds great, doesn't it? But it is absolutely meaningless. It doesn't mean anything whatsoever. It's just a lot of buzzwords that have been put together to try and make you sound good and the assessors will see through it straight away.

Don't think for one moment that you can use 'Buzzword Bingo.'

4. Describing what you generally do as opposed to a specific occasion

What the questions will invariably ask for is, 'can you tell us about a specific occasion when….?' It needs to be specific. They ask for a specific example - it needs to be specific about one incident in time, not what you generally do. Don't generalise, because if you do give an answer where you generalise, it will score zero. It'll score absolutely zero.

5. Spelling mistakes, and your word count.

Here's an example for you from a form right in front of me! A client who is claiming to have used their 'imitative' instead of their initiative. Make sure that you've got the right word! Get other people to read it and if it makes no sense get them to tell you.

When I read this and the person was saying, 'I used my imitative' I had to start thinking, 'what's that mean?' Then I worked it out, "oh, they actually mean initiative.' Well, you'll get marked down for that because that is a spelling mistake. It's a grammatical error. Make sure your sentence makes sense. There are so many sentences I've read out aloud on past forms where I just don't understand the contents. They don't flow. The commas aren't in the right place or there are no commas at all, or there are no full stops. Or the first word of a sentence is not in capital. Spelling mistakes everywhere. You can fail based on spelling mistakes and grammatical errors alone. Please make sure you get these things right. Ask someone else to look at it. Ask me to look at it. I'm more expensive than a friend or relative, but I will go through the whole of the application form and make sure it's good to go and give you really, really detailed feedback because I know what they're looking for.

The people, your friends, and family may not know what they're looking for, but still utilise them. Read it out to yourself. Get them to read it out loud. You'll realise how some of the sentences and some of the phrases that you've used, just make no sense whatsoever, or that you need more commas or semicolons or full stops. That your grammar is all over the place. Please get this right folks.

6. Motivation without cliches!

All right, so this is where the form moves into motivations as opposed to the competency type questions that they ask you. The motivation and inspiration for wanting to be a police officer type question. One of them asks you for your motivation. What's motivating you to want to be a police officer? Why do you want to be a police officer? Tough questions to answer – the following are phrases used from real application forms. They're ones that you should definitely not use because you will fail just based on these phrases.

Here's the first one:

'Unfortunately, I no longer like my current job and I'm looking for a greater challenge.' That's the reason why you want to be a police officer? Because you don't like what you're doing anymore? No, you're not joining our Constabulary.

'My personality, values, and qualities are similar to those of the police service.' Frankly this is just a waste of words.

'I feel I will be able to make a positive contribution.' Well, that's wonderful. What's inspiring you to want to make a positive contribution?

'No two days are the same.' Yeah, we know that but that's not actually telling me why you want to be a police officer.
'I want to use my experience and skills to adapt to various challenges.' Absolutely meaningless. What experiences? What skills? How will they enable to meet those challenges and what would those challenges be?

'I want to help save lives and generally help people.' Well, go into the medical profession. Go into so many other professions that where you can save lives and generally help people. It's just vague and cliched and won't get you any marks whatsoever.

'I want to make communities a safer place to live and reduce crime.' A worthy objective but vague, cliched, and meaningless. You don't have much of a word count so make sure that you use it wisely.

The last one, 'I'd find it incredibly exciting.' Well, yeah, I'm sure you will but that's not the reason why you want to be a police officer.

What I advocate instead is making the answer personal to you. What is your real motivation? Who or what initially motivated you or inspired you to want to be a police officer? That's your starting point and then we do something called a timeline. What have you done to further that interest in the police until you've got to the point where you applied today?

Avoid the cliches. Avoid all the vague statements. I don't know where people get them from. I suspect there are books out there that tell you to say these things, but the assessors have heard it all before.

And please do not start off your answer with, 'I've always wanted to be a police officer.' No, you haven't. You weren't six months old and always wanting to be a police officer, were you? 'From an early age, I wanted to be a police officer.' Please, give me a break.

Okay, then we move on to questions about why you've chosen this force:

'I've lived here all my life.' Some people begin and end on that. That is not the reason why you want to apply to your force.

'I value the cultural differences in the area that I live in.' Really, that's nice for you but that's still not answering the question.

'I believe this force area is a good mix of town city and countryside, therefore it would be a good place for me to work.' In every county or city area in the country there is a 'good mix.' Even the Metropolitan Police has countryside-based officers.

'The values of this force are the same as mine.' Oh, please give me a break. What a cliché! It's not actually answering the question.

Think about what's unique about the force. Think about why you would want to actually be a member of this force and that might involve you actually talking to police officers and getting evidence from them where they will tell you that it feels like a family.

'I feel incredibly well supported every day when I've met a challenge or a difficulty. Someone's been there to help me.' No, just no! Make your answer really, really individual. Make it something that stands out for you in terms of why you want to join that constabulary. I've lived here all my life. Really? That's lovely for you but it's not going to get you into this Constabulary.

7. What do police officers do?

The next question that's asked on the standard application form is:

'In detail, what sort of tasks do you feel you are going to be undertaking as a police officer?'

The following is an answer from a client that would not have worked out for him (we sorted it following my advice!):

'What sort of tasks, I'm going to work in a team. I'm going to be reassuring the public. I'm going to be engaging with the public. I'm going to be taking statements. I'll be keeping the peace. I'll use my initiative. I'll be solving problems. There will be various laws to follow and laws to learn.'

All of this is too vague - it is the sort of thing that I get to read often – without my support the individuals concerned would have failed at application form stage. Why? Because the question is asking for detail!

Find out what detailed things the police do. What in detail do they do? Arresting people, most of the application forms I see never mention the fact that you be arresting people. But what sort of people? What sort of stop and searches will you be doing? What are the crimes that are prevalent in the area? Do you know of the crimes that are associated with County Lines? Do you even know what County Lines is? Will you be dealing with domestic violence incidents? Will you be dealing with sudden deaths? You're going to have to come across people who are dead and that passed away. Road traffic collisions where people have suffered serious harm?

Start thinking that it's not just about how, 'I'll be investigating crime.' What sorts of crime will you be investigating primarily in your first few years? What sort of things will you be dealing with on a day-to-day basis? Get the detail in. One of the best ways of doing that is to follow officers on social media. At the right time, get in touch with them and ask if you can just have 15 minutes of their time where you just ask them the question, 'what sort of things do you deal with? Can you give me some detail?' And then you can use their answers to help you generate your own. That is great research.

Whatever you do, do not use vague statements.

8. The impact of being a Police Officer on your personal life?

Another question you may be asked is, 'what sort of impact is being a police officer going to have on your personal life?' This is a common interview question as well because they want to make sure that you really, really understand exactly what impact being a police officer will have on your personal life.

Do not make the claim that it won't have an impact, because straight away if you say that, I will know that you do not understand what the impact is going to be on you. That you will be a police officer, you'll have to work shifts and you might miss some family events or parties. You might have to go on holiday at different times. These are all things that my nine-year-old son could tell me, so it's not detailed enough. It really isn't detailed enough. And you definitely do not say how I might lose some friends, because the first question I'm thinking then is what sort of friends are you keeping? Your friends should be proud of you. 'I might lose friends.' Well, I'm a bit concerned about the sort of friends that you're keeping so don't say that.

Instead, think about the real impact it's going to have on your life. Talk with your family and evidence that you've talked with your family and your friends. It is going to have a massive impact on you. It's going to have a massive impact on your mental health. Physically, it's going to have an impact on you. Not just physically as in exhausted and feeling run down at times because you're working shifts, but also physically as and some people might try and hurt you. This is something that's going to impact on your personal life. They want a very personal account from you as to how you feel it will impact on your personal life.

9. How have you been preparing for the recruitment process? (Reading this book is not the answer!!)

Okay, one of the next questions is, 'what sort of preparation have you undertaken to prepare for this role.' You answer needs to be specific. I mean, what they're looking for is specific evidence. Just saying, 'I've spoken to police officers,' is not enough. Great that you did, but what did you learn? Which police officers were they and what did you learn as a result of this?

'I've researched being a police officer and it's very interesting.' What research did you do? Why do you find it interesting?

'I've looked at the website.' So has everyone else. So what?

'I've attended an event put on by the force to tell me all about being a police officer.' Yeah, so has everyone else. What have you done over and beyond what everyone else has done? I've done some research. What sort of research?

'I've got myself fit.' What have you done to get fit?

Bottom line - make your answers unique to you and don't be utilising all those cliches.

10. Be a people person who gives 120% without being asked to do so!

This is the last top tip for you, the last piece of guidance. In the answers you provide about the experiences in your life, you should be able to give examples of when you've given 120% effort without being asked to do so. Using examples where you've been tasked to do something is not going to score very highly because you would just have to do it anyway. You're not showing anything remarkable. You're not showing your initiative. You're just demonstrating that you can do what you're told to do. Examples that involve people work well because being a police officer is a very people orientated job. You will be dealing with people, and working with people, and collaborating with people, and solving problems with people from the moment you walk out of the locker room, until the moment you hang up your keys and go back into the locker room.

Everything else in between is working with other people, so use examples that involve other people. Use examples where you've challenged yourself, where you really pushed yourself. Where things didn't go right the first time. And that's fine, if you challenge yourself, you need to accept that the actions you are taking are rarely going to be perfect. They will never be perfect. Once we build up that action taking momentum and every day, we are doing something that's taken us closer to our goal, we also know that the action we're taking is not always going to be perfect. It's imperfect action, but the beauty of that is you can look back on it, learn from it and think, 'what can I do better?'

Challenge yourself, take on additional responsibilities, push your limits, then push yourself beyond those limits. Make mistakes and learn from those mistakes. I know it sounds like a magnificent cliche but please do put yourself in situations where you've got the opportunity to make mistakes. Try things out. They won't always work. The more you exercise those 'challenge muscles' by pushing yourself and taking on further responsibility, the more it will get easier to do and the more evidence you will gather for your answers. This is how to get awesome for the process - not just for your application form, but also at the assessment centre, and at your final interview.

It doesn't matter how old you are as you can apply to join the police at 17. And I know some people may say, 'yeah, but you've not got enough life experience at that age.' Well, that's not a barrier, otherwise, they wouldn't have introduced the lower age limit of 17. As long as you're 18 when you're walking through the door, and you get your warrant card. That's all they're looking for. Think about the opportunities you can create for yourself. Get involved in volunteering. Get involved in Duke of Edinburgh. Get involved in the Scouts or Guides. Get involved in volunteer organisations. Get involved in your part-time job. Push yourself. Ask for further responsibility. Ask to take some of the weight off your manager or supervisor and ask if you could take on some of their roles. It doesn't matter how old you are as long as you're capable of doing it. Push, push, push yourself. Ask for more responsibility. Use your initiative. Try things out. Give 120% without being asked to do so.

That's what they're looking for. They're looking for promise, they're not looking for someone who's got so much life experience that they're going to be perfect in every way (they do not exist!!). They're looking for someone who's got promise. This is what your application form needs to reflect folks. Make sure that you don't make any of the errors that I've just outlined here. Make sure you do exactly what I've outlined, and your application form should sail through.

Now, I know I have mentioned this before, but the importance of the application form, I can't overstress it. It's not a formality. The police don't owe you a living. They're not going to give you a warrant card on a silver platter. You're going to have to earn it and the application form is your first contact with the force where you can demonstrate that you're exactly the sort of person that they are looking for.

A lot of forces will screen people out based on application forms. They will screen out thousands. If they've got 5,000 applications, there's no way they can provide 5,000 assessment centres and interviews for all those applications. They will whittle that down to about a thousand or even less. Depending on supply and demand, they could mark the application forms really hard. You might be thinking I prepared all my life for this. I've been in the Special Constabulary. I've been a cadet. I've done this, I've done the other. But if your application form doesn't reflect exactly what they're looking for, you will fail.

It's so important that we focus on this. That's why in the earlier chapter I've given you the application form questions. Not just the national College of Policing questions, but also the sort of questions forces that have ditched the national application form use. That's why it's so important that you start preparing now. Some of you might be thinking how that's a lot of hard work. Yes, it is. Like I said, no one's going to hand a warrant card to you on a silver platter. You've got to work hard for it.

But the good thing is you're in the right company. I know I've said this before, but if you are prepared to work hard, I'll show you what to do. You've got to do the hard work. I will show you what you need to do. You're not going to get through this by osmosis. You're not going to get through this by some magic bullet because there isn't one. There is no quick easy way to get into the police. It requires hard work and determination from you. This is where it starts folks.

Make a difference. Get through this first time and then in the next chapters, we're going to talk about things like the assessment centres and the interview phase. Then beyond that, there's fitness, vetting medical... There's a lot of stages to get through but I'll help you get there. It might take a year or two but I'm here to help you get through it all.

So, folks, I hope you enjoyed this chapter. Please do ask me any questions if you have anything that you're unsure about. You can get in touch with me via the Facebook groups using Messenger. Or you could just drop me a line at the email address for Bluelight, which is info@bluelightconsultancy.com.

https://bluelightonline.co.uk/book

Chapter 8 - Values, Corporate Knowledge and Awareness. The Impact of Being a Police Officer on Your Personal Life

In this chapter, we're going to take a look at values, your corporate knowledge and awareness, and the impact on your personal life. So that's three different types of questions, but I'm not going to spend a huge amount of time on each one of them, which is why I pulled them all into just one chapter.

So one of the questions you might get asked on your application form or interview is:

'What values are important to a police officer?'

Or you might also get asked:

'What values are important to you?'

Or:

'What values are important to you, which you feel might be beneficial as a police officer?'

So, there are all sorts of different values questions you can get asked. It's really important here that you answer this question with authenticity because anyone can just reel off some of the values from the Competency and Values Framework. Of course, you need to be aware of what the Competency and Values Framework is, and you need to be aware of the values and the competencies within it. But if you simply start off your answer with, 'The values that are important to police officers are Impartiality, Public Service, Integrity, and Transparency,' then you're just going to sound like someone who's just repeating exactly what is in the CVF. It's going to sound like you've swallowed the CVF, and I know that that really annoys interviewers. I know that because I used to be one of them.

Have any of you have seen the webinar I ran with the retired Chief Constable Andy Cook from Merseyside police (he wasn't quite retired when I ran the webinar)? Actually, he's my old friend and colleague, as I joined with him 36 years ago. He was the last officer standing from my intake and he said exactly the same thing. His advice for anyone who's going to join the police, or for anyone who's seeking promotion, or going for specialist interviews is to be completely authentic, to talk from your heart, and to talk from what is emotionally you as opposed to just rattling off a 'load of CVFs,' as he said. I know there are other chief constables who hold the same view. Nick Adderley from Northamptonshire Constabulary, a fine chief constable, ex-Greater Manchester police. He's put this out on Twitter, how in their promotion interviews, they are looking for something about that person, not someone who can just reel off phrases from the Competency and Values Framework. So, it's important that you don't just do that. That you are genuinely authentic with your answer.

I'll give you an example of this. Recently in a one-to-one practice interview, one of my clients started off with that - they started off with, 'Transparency, Integrity, Public Service and Impartiality. Those are the values important to a police officer, and those are values that are important to me, and I'm aligned with the values that are important to the Police Service.'

Oh, dear!

No, no, no! So, I said, 'Alright. Okay, Brendan to... (the name of the individual), honesty time, tell me what's really important to you. What value would other people say is the strongest within you?' And as quick as anything he said, 'Compassion.' Well, compassion is not in the Competency and Values Framework - that was my challenge back to him, and he said, 'no, but that's the thing that people would say about me, and that's the thing I know that's important to me. It's to always be compassionate to others, especially people who may not have had the same opportunities as me.' Brilliant, that's what we're looking for. He then went on to give an example of when he had been compassionate to someone. He used this in his final interview with his chosen force and went onto pass!

Being compassionate is a value. Being selfless is a value. It's just not in the Competency and Values Framework. Now, I don't want you all going off now and saying, 'I believe compassion is my greatest value.' Or, 'I believe selflessness is my greatest value and one that will be beneficial to the police service.' Because you need to be ready for the next question which is, 'Great. So, selflessness is important to you, and you believe that be important to the Police Service. Can you give me an example of when you've been selfless?' You need to be ready for that. There are ways of answering that question which I go into in far more depth in my interview course, and especially in my one-to-one coaching and the webinars that go with the online course. So that's an introduction to values covered. Make sense?

So the next thing I want to discuss with you is corporate knowledge - your corporate awareness. Now, my expectation is that you will have a massive awareness of the police service and the challenges that they face so that you can be prepared for the question, 'What challenges do we face at this moment in time?'

And so, what I'd like you to research - and again on my online course and the webinars, we go into this in far, far more detail, is this. So, I'm going give you loads of links and places to look, but I'll give you some clues here as well. So, for the national, you'd be wanting to look at the National Police Chief's Council and their vision for 2025. You'll also be wanting to take a look at the work of the National Crime Agency. There's plenty of other organisations that can give you an insight into what the current issues are, like the Police Foundation and Policing Insight magazine, which is online, and Police Professional magazine, which is also online. Now, those two magazines are subscription services. However, they do also offer lots of articles for free.

Now we are going to drill it down to force level. So, this is where you're going to research what challenges the force faces. Your first thought might be things like austerity. That is a big challenge, but it's not really demonstrating that you've got an insight into the real challenges that that force faces. Every Force has unique challenges to them. Some of those challenges are shared, such as dealing with vulnerable people, and mental health issues, but others are unique to that particular force.

So, for example, the Greater Manchester Police does not have a problem with County Lines, as in drug dealers and organised criminality trying to get a stake into Greater Manchester Police's area to set up those County Lines. Instead, they're the ones who export that problem to forces like Cheshire and North Wales. So, I'd expect you to be fully aware of what County Lines are and how they impact on your force.

I'd also expect you to be able to talk eloquently about Adverse Childhood Experiences. I'd expect you to know exactly what the Chief Constable has been saying in the news, in the media. I'd expect you to be setting up Google Alerts for all sorts of different phrases, so that every day, when a certain phrase is mentioned in the media, or in a blog, or elsewhere, actually, anywhere on the internet, you will get a link to the article, or the blog, or whatever it might be where that phrase was mentioned.

There are several different things you can do here, but the first thing I do is just set up a Google Alert for the name of the Chief Constable of the force that you want to join. And make sure you know the name of your Chief Constable! Know the name of your Policing and Crime Commissioner! This is another thing I do in my webinars; I spend a short 5 to 10 minutes looking at everyone's corporate knowledge, and invariably about half of the individuals on the webinars don't know the name of the Chief Constable or the name of the Policing and Crime Commissioner, never mind what they've been saying in the media recently.

So, this is how you ensure you've got corporate knowledge, that you've got the local police and national police issues and challenges in your DNA. You need to be prepared for the question, 'tell me what the challenges are?' Then be ready for a really tough follow up question, 'can you tell me how you believe you will be able to assist us in meeting those challenges?' So that's quite a tough question for you there. You need to be ready for it as one of the questions that we practice in the webinars and could be asked in your interview.

The third part of this chapter is the impact on your personal life. This is an important question because you need to persuade the interviewer that you are really, aware of the sort of challenges that you're going to face as a police officer, the full impact it's going to have on your personal life.

So, if you start off by saying, 'I've worked shifts before, so I don't think it's going to have any impact,' then you are wrong!

'I've talked about it with my family. I've researched the role. I don't think it's going to have an impact on me.' Again - wrong. It is going to have an impact on you. I can absolutely promise you this. There is no one who's joined the police where it's not had an impact on their personal life. They might tell you that it hasn't, but it has. I absolutely guarantee that it's had an impact on their personal life, and quite a big impact as well.

So simply saying, 'I've got to work shifts. I might work and miss some holidays. I might miss some family events.' It's all a bit superficial. I'd start off with that, but then I'd jump into talking about the real, real impact it's going to have on your personal life.

And do not say, 'I might lose some friends.' The number of people who have said that to me in one-to-ones and in the webinars, and then straight away I followed it up with, 'So you said in your answer there that you might lose some friends because you're going to be a police officer. What sort of friends do you keep?' And this just completely floors them. They get floored by that. So don't say you're going to lose some friends because of being a police officer!

Now, the really difficult thing to do is to research this answer and to be able to talk about the emotional, mental, and physical impact being a police officer is going to have on your life. There are no right or wrong answers here, but they just want you to recognise what that emotional, mental, and physical impact is going to be.

How are you going to manage going home to your family, or friends, or your loved ones after a horrendous 13, 14-hour night shift, where you signed up for a 12-hour one, but it turned into 13 or 14 hours. Where the last incident you attended was a sudden death of a six-week-old baby?

By then you've already attended all sorts of incidents before that, things that people aren't even aware that happens in the world. You've got this amazing privilege, this amazing honour of serving Her Majesty - because that's what you are. You're a Crown Servant and in a position where her emblem is on your uniform. And you are out there dealing with things that communities and individuals don't even realise happen, and nor should they. You are there to protect them from those things, and to deal with those difficult things when they happen. But that's not going to happen without it having some kind of impact on your life.

So I'd like you to take a look at the sort of post-traumatic stress disorder that being a police officer can cause. I'd like you to look at organisations like Oscar Kilo, who are doing a lot of research around well-being for police officers. Also, look at the work of the Police Federation in respect of well-being. From all of this, you'll be able to formulate answers that talk about the emotional and mental strain that it's going to have on you and on your family. Because how are you going to answer the question when you get back home from your shift and one of your loved ones says, 'So how was your night?' What do you say to them? Do you say to them that only a couple of hours ago, 'I was checking a dead six-week-old baby for any signs of malicious intent while I've got a grieving family behind me asking, why are you taking the clothes off their little baby girl?' This is tough. It's really difficult. How are you going to answer those questions?

This is something to think about. If you don't think about this and you just come out with the superficial 'shifts, holidays, lose friends' answer, then there's every chance you're going to score very poorly on that answer. There's every chance they're not going to take you on until you've got that real dawning realisation of the real impact it's going to have. But it's not all negative, because there's a lot of support out there for you as well. Take a look and research the support that's provided for you.

And then, there's also the physical impact - it's going to wear you out. You are going to be working at times when your body was meant to be sleeping, and that's going to have an impact on you. In your early 20s you could be zapping around at night-time, and you'd be thinking what's all the fuss about. I remember I was like that in my 20s. Night shifts? They weren't a problem but as you get older, it gets harder. Trust me. It gets harder. Once you're in your 40s, it starts getting harder to work those night shifts. They start to have more of an impact on you. Your sleep patterns get disturbed. Actually, you don't really have a sleep pattern as a police officer.

Also, think about the chances of you being assaulted. At some point, someone's going to assault you. I guarantee that. There's just no getting away from it. At some point, someone's either going to try or they're going to succeed in assaulting you. It might be a minor assault, or it might be (I hope not) a more serious one. But the statistics tell us of a really high percentage, and this is increasing, of police officers are getting assaulted. So certainly, that's going to happen. Now, you've got your protective equipment to support you. You've got your colleagues to support you. You've got all the training that you're going to get to help you avoid those sorts of situations. But sometime in the future, it will happen.

How are you going to deal with that? How are you going to explain to yourself how someone wanted to harm you? How are you going to explain the scratches, the bruises, the cuts? How can you explain that to your family? And then how are they going to react when you then go to work next? You don't think your loved ones aren't going to worry about you, do you? Because they are.

Now, on my course and in my webinars, I always end on a positive note. There is one thing, one thing that's going to absolutely nail the 'Impact' answer. I'm going to tease you a little bit here. If you want to find out what that one thing is, then I'd invite you to join me on my courses. Join me on my webinars because that one thing is the one that puts the icing on the cake for this answer. It's one that you probably have realised, actually, you may not have realised just yet until I mention it, in which case then you'll go, 'Ah, wow. That's the perfect, perfect ending.'

So, if you'd like to be able to articulate an answer to the 'Impact' question, my invitation is, 'Join us.' Go to the Offer Wall that's part of this book and join us on one of the webinars and get to practice with me. Get to practice personally with me - there is no substitute for that. There's no substitute for that kind of in-depth preparation that you're going to get with me on those webinars. It will, I promise you, make a huge difference in your preparation.

So there you go, folks. I hope you've enjoyed that chapter and got a lot out of it. I hope it's now got you thinking about what research you need to do now. If in the last chapter you were thinking, 'phew, I thought I had to do a lot of preparation for the online assessment centre." You might now be thinking, I've got so much more to do for the final interview." Then you're right. You're absolutely right.

Preparation and practice - rehearse the answers to these questions. Get to the point where you can speak eloquently, confidently, from the heart, and make it conversational in your interview. I know you've heard me say this before, but this is the way forward.

Practice, practice, practice, practice.

Every day, take some action that's going to take you closer to your goal of being a police officer. The rehearsal should not be on the day. We rehearse these sorts of questions and the answers to these questions, so that on the day, we can come across as being prepared, confident, and conversational. I promise you that is the way to succeed and get a high mark at your interview so that you can guarantee a place on the next intake. As opposed to what some forces do, which is to put the lowest-scoring candidates who have passed on an intake that might be up to two years away.

I know you might be thinking, 'Surely, that doesn't happen.' Yes, it does. People who have already spent well over a year in the application process getting start dates almost two years from that point. I know people who've been given a start date, which is 22 months away from their Final Interview result!

22 months away! And they already spent a year in the application or recruitment process. So that's almost 3 years from the point they picked up an application form to the point where they get in. That's almost 3 years!

I'll say this again, and it's with the very best intention. It's to get you to a level where you are performing far higher than all the other candidates. Because what the forces will do is they'll put those high-performing candidates into the next intake so their joining date might be just six months away, right? It could be four months away, could even be two or three months away. They'll speed you through vetting medical and fitness because they want you.

They still want the others who don't score quite as well, but who knows what the future is going to hold? Who knows what funding issues they're going to have? Because they might tell you that the proposed intake is going to be 22 months away. I've never seen anything beyond 22 months by the way. They may tell you that, but they could always cancel the intake. They could always just write to you even a month before, or as one force did, 3 weeks before an intake started, to say, 'actually, we're not running that intake now. Thank you for your interest. Goodbye.' So, we're going to avoid that folks. Nothing is certain until you're walking through the door, and you've got that warrant card in your pocket. Nothing is certain. It needs hard work. It needs dedication all the way through the process.

So I'm here to help you with that. That's what I do. I do that and provide that support. I provide that guidance. I provide that holding hand that's going to get you to that point. Join me and I'll help you. I'll keep inspiring you. I'll drive you on those days when you're thinking, 'I can't do this anymore.' It's going to be Brendan in the back of your mind pushing you on. That's what I do. I've done that for thousands and thousands. Let me do that for you as well.

https://bluelightonline.co.uk/book

Chapter 9 - Situational Judgement Tests

In one of the last chapters, we looked at an overview of the whole of the recruitment process and how it can vary from force to force. Now I'm going to focus on an aspect of the assessment and recruitment process that most of you will go through, which is the Online Assessment Centre.

At the time of writing, and certainly until March 2022, and maybe beyond, what is ahead of you is the Online Assessment Centre, run, administered, and designed by the College of Policing. The first part of that is a Situational Judgment Test. Now, I say the first part of it, as the Situational Judgment Test is the first part for some forces, and for other forces, it isn't.

I know, confusing. Some forces choose to do their own form of Situational Judgment Test. And these can be called different things, it could be called a 'Behavioural Assessment' and all sorts of other different titles, but they all follow pretty much the same process. So, what they're doing here is to put you into situations that you may be in as a future police officer. And they're going to ask you out of four options, which one do you think is the best? You also might have to rank them if it's the force's own system. Why the College of Policing let some forces use their own funky systems I don't know, but it is what it is, and you've just got to get over it.

Some forces have decided not to do any Situational Judgment Test at all and just put people straight through to Stage Two of the Online Assessment Centre. So, Stage 2 is the interview and Stage 3 is the Written and Briefing exercise. First though, for the rest of you, you've got to get through Stage 1, which is the Situational Judgment Test.

What I'm going to do next is to blow a few myths out the water. And these are the myths that the College of Policing give you because you're going to get 12 questions and they're all multiple choice. And as I said before, they're going to put you in situations where you would have to work out what would you do as a police officer.

But what they're also going to say to you is that you should answer the questions as honestly as possible, act naturally, and just be yourself.

All these three pieces of advice are the worst thing to do.

It's honestly the worst thing to do and I'm going to prove it to you. So, in my online course, that's the one that you can purchase on its own, or you can purchase it with the online course plus webinar version where you get to practice with me, I have modules that will prepare you for the Situational Judgement Test.

By the way, there's no better person to practice with than me! If you want to access this kind of support, then the Offer Wall that comes as part of this book (link at the end of every chapter) has amazing price reductions and bonuses. In that Offer Wall, you'll find an amazing offer to purchase the webinar version of the OAC course (Gold Package) and get to work personally with me.

So, I've got some sample questions I can share with you that at this moment in time. Pay attention to these as not one of my clients has come back to say, 'I've failed Stage 1 of the Online Assessment Centre.' That's down to my practice questions and guidance. If you do fail, by the way, that's it. You are automatically failed for the whole process. You can't go through to Stage 2. If you do pass, and you will pass it if you're one of my clients, you go straight through to the Stage 2 which is the interview. But you go through to it straight away.

So, you need to be ready for Stage 2 unless you're doing the In Force Situational Judgment Test, in which case, you'll have to wait. You'll be told that you've passed and then you'll have to wait for the joining instructions for the College of Policing Stage 2.

All right, so let me give you an example of a Situational Judgement Test question. So, I said before that the last thing you need to do is to act naturally, be yourself, and just be honest in your answers. I'm going to prove now that this is poor advice and the way I'm going to do that is I'm going to give you a question from my sample Situational Judgment Test bank. I'm going to give you a question one from that. I'm going to ask you to answer this question as honestly as possible, being yourself and acting naturally. So as the real genuine honest acting naturally person you are today.

How would you answer this question?

Your colleague who you know very well approaches you. He explains that he's currently working on a case within his team and has found out that there is a registered sex offender living next door to you. Your colleague explains how this is confidential information, which shouldn't be shared with you, but they wanted to warn you for the safety of your family as this is a high-risk individual. You know that this is a breach of Data Protection and GDPR.

So do you:

- A. Thank your colleague for sharing this information, important information with you, understand that your colleague was trying to help you and your family

- B. Explain to your colleague that you understand he was trying to help you but highlight that this is a breach of GDPR and Data Protection, and you should not do it again.
- C. Immediately report your colleague for this breach of The Code of Ethics to your sergeant.

D. Highlight to your sergeant that someone is breaching GDPR but refrain from being specific about who it is. Your colleague was trying to help you, so you don't want to get them into trouble.

Does that make sense so far?

So essentially, you've got a situation where one of your colleagues has given you information that one of your neighbours is a registered sex offender, because of a case they're working on. You should not be entitled to have that data. You shouldn't be in possession of it because it is in breach of Data Protection. It is in breach because they are not sharing that information with you for a genuine, authentic policing purpose. So, the choices are, do you thank them because they're just trying to do the best for you, thank them but give him a warning and say, 'look, don't do that again mate, you could get into trouble.' Or do you C. Go straight to your sergeant and 'grass' them up. Or do you D. Go to your sergeant and say, 'sarge, I need to let you know that someone's breaching GDPR, but I'm not prepared to say who they are because I might get into trouble.'

So think about who you are now, and bear in mind, there's no thought police out there. So, answer this question in your head as honestly as you can, acting naturally, as you would be now, and being your true authentic self. How would you answer that question, which option would you take? I'll give you a moment to think about that.

All right, my guess is that most of you have gone for B. Because in the real world, would you go straight to your boss and say, 'boss, my best friend, one of my colleagues, has just breached GDPR knowing that they can actually get the sack for it?' They could be dismissed for this. Would you, really?

Most people, and I know this because I've run this exercise on my interactive webinars with hundreds and hundreds of my clients, 90% plus of them will say B. I'll thank him but then I'll give him a warning. There are less than 10% also who say C, which is go straight to my sergeant and grass them up. I shouldn't use that phrase, grass them up, but tell on them, report them to my sergeant. These individuals invariably are PCSOs, special constables, or people who already work in an environment where Data Protection is important and where they must be really guarded about how they share information and who they share information with. A smaller percentage say D, that they'd go to their Sergeant to report that someone has been breaching GDPR and Data Protection, but they're not prepared to say who. Very few go for the A, just thank him, and do nothing else.

So, you probably know already what the answer is that they're looking for. The answer, the correct answer is C, that you would go to your sergeant and report this straight away. Why? Because of The Code of Ethics. The Code of Ethics makes it really clear that should you become aware of any misconduct, you are required to question the individual about it, challenge them about what they've said or done, and then report it to someone who is senior to you.

There's no if's and but's. The Code of Ethics is the legislation of our land. It is an Act of Parliament. And it is a requirement, it's not a request, it's not guidance. It is a requirement. So, if you fail to do that, you are committing misconduct as well, and you could find yourself being dismissed. Now, that's not the case in most employments.

For most employments, a lot of employers would welcome you giving your colleague a warning. It doesn't work like that in the police though. This is a Code of Ethics. This is the law of our land, and this individual has broken the law. So, it's really quite serious misconduct, although it may not seem it, on the surface. So, C is the correct answer. B is generally what most people will do.

So, folks that's how the Situational Judgment Test works. The guidance I'm going to give you is one, to jump on my webinars, of course, and we'll practice these things and there is no better person to practice with than me. Two, just think very carefully about how you're going to approach the situations. Don't approach them by being honest in your answers, do not approach them by acting naturally, do not approach them by just being yourself. Approach them as if you were the best version of your future Constable self you could ever, ever be. Does that make sense?

Approach every question as if you are the best version of your future Constable self. One that complies with every regulation, every rule, where The Code of Ethics is in your DNA. You are the best version of your future Constable self. This is how you pass the Situational Judgment Test. Knowing or reading your competencies is not going to help you. It'll just confuse you, especially when you get to that 'Wheel of Confusion.'

Following my guidance will. Remember, they're looking for people who are going to be capable of making decisions, people who are going to problem-solve with other organisations, people who put the needs of others before their own needs, consistently and all the time, people who will challenge inappropriate behaviour, no matter who the individual is, who's committed the inappropriate behaviour, they will challenge it, question it, and report it as per The Code of Ethics.

Is this making sense, folks?

You might be thinking, 'That's not me yet.' Well of course it's not you yet, because they're looking for potential and that's what these Situational Judgment Tests are looking for. Have you got the potential? So, follow my guidance, do the practice SJTs that come as part of the course, and you will pass. And I can say that with confidence because not one of my clients has ever come back and said, 'I failed SJTs and didn't go any further.' Not one.

Now, there may be one or two out there, who've not told me, but those would be the ones who have not followed my guidance, they've not done the work, they've not done the practice SJTs, they've not thought about each one of the answers, have not reviewed it to discover, 'right, that's why I should have put C, instead of B.'

The majority of my clients are the individuals who are going to pass. They're prepared to do the hard work I set them, and they will reap the benefits, which is a pass.

So, there you go, folks, Situational Judgment Tests in a nutshell. That's all there is to them. But you've just got to, like I said before, do not accept the advice or the guidance from the College of Policing, accept my advice instead. And you're not doing anything unethical here. You're just pretending to be the best version of your future Constable self. Why wouldn't you? That's what they're assessing you against. Why not be that person?

So, I hope you enjoyed this chapter folks and hopefully it's got you in the right mindset to do the Situational Judgment Test. If you would like to join the interactive webinars with me, with me where I guarantee you will pass, or you get your money back, you get a full refund, then go to the Offer Wall, which is at the end of every chapter, and you will see an amazing offer to purchase the Gold Package.

The Gold Package is the one where you get to work with me in a small group. They are awesome. I love running those webinars. So come and join me. Come and join me and guarantee your success at this stage.

https://bluelightonline.co.uk/book

Chapter 10 - Stage 2 of the Online Assessment Centre

In this chapter, we're going to take a look at Stage 2 of the Online Assessment Centre and what that involves. I'm going to give you a bit of a teaser, a bit of a clue as to some of the questions you're going to get in this assessment to help prepare you for the process.

Now let's just get this one out of the way, although the College of Policing calls Stage 2 an interview, it's not an interview. That might seem a bit confusing, bear with me.

So an interview is normally where an interviewer asks a candidate questions and the candidate responds, and where if the candidate is not quite sure about something, the interviewer might probe a little bit more and ask further questions and guide the candidate along the journey so that the candidate has got the opportunity to demonstrate the best version of themselves that they can be.

It's the interviewer's job to put them at ease and to get from them exactly what they're looking for in the ideal candidate.

Stage 2 is not that.

it is completely automated.

This is where you're going to sign in, log on, and you're going to be introduced to a screen that's going to give you some instructions and there'll be a person in the background giving you some instructions.

It's a video, they're not really there.

And what they're going to tell you that's going to happen is, that you're going to be asked five questions. Three of them are value-based questions on Integrity, Public Service, and Transparency from the Competency and Values Framework. And two competencies, We Take Ownership and, We are Innovative and Open-Minded.

You'll be asked to press the start button and when you press that start button, a woman will appear on the screen. It's currently a woman. She will ask you the first question, and then once she's finished asking that question, you've got one minute to think about your answer and make any notes that you might want to refer to in your answer. And then as soon as that minute is up, you then have five minutes to deliver your answer.

Now some of you might be thinking, 'five minutes, that's not long.' But if your answer isn't structured enough and isn't detailed enough you are going to get to about two minutes and have not much else to say. You're just going to watch the timer ticking away until it gets to five minutes, and then you move on to the next one.

Again, you're going get asked a question. You've got one minute to think about it and make notes, and then deliver your five-minute answer.

That pattern goes on for all the five questions.

Like I said, Integrity, Public Service, Transparency, We Take Ownership, and We are Innovative and Open-Minded. Whether they go in that order or not, I do not know. It doesn't really matter because you're going to be super prepared. That's why it doesn't matter.

So let's see what else I can tell you about that process. Yeah, there's no test of your motivation or value. So don't be thinking here that, I want to really deliver this sense of who I am and why they should recruit me. Because the assessors who are assessing don't really care. What happens is they get in their inbox all the video recordings of your interview, an upload to their inbox, and they just assess them. They don't know what force you're applying to, nor do they probably care. I've worked for and with the College of Policing on four occasions, and on the last occasion when I was working in their Organisational Development Team as an associate, I met fellow associates who also did assessing.

More than half of them had never had a warrant card in their pockets, so they've never been police officers. The College of Policing uses all sorts of people to do the interview assessments. They're all appropriately qualified to assess your answer. All suitably experienced to assess your answer, but think about it, they're listening to these answers' day in day out. They are not thinking anything about whether this person really wants to join the police or not. They are not wondering as to whether they can really sense your motivation to join, because they're not scoring against that. They're scoring you against the behavioural statements that are from each one of the values and competencies.

It is frankly, one of the most formulaic tick-box approaches I've ever seen in police recruitment. I joined in 1985 when it certainly wasn't anything like tick box. Three days and two nights in the Welsh mountains, being 'beasted' through a variety of different and very big, peculiar exercises that were certainly not formulaic. This is the opposite - completely formulaic. It's so formulaic I could coach my 13-year-old daughter to pass this. I would put money on it that she would pass. Because all you need to do is describe in detail in a structured way how you dealt with certain problems, how you dealt with certain issues in a five-minute window.

My daughter could do that. She could describe a time when she's managed and supported change. She could... that's the Innovative and Open-Minded question by the way. She could talk about difficult decisions - that's the Transparency question. She could talk about doing the right thing even when doing nothing was the easier option, that's Integrity. Then she could talk about how she's taken ownership for resolving problems and working with others to do so. She can also talk about times when she's delivered an awesome service in terms of some of the things she's done to raise money for charity. And she's only 13! I'm quite confident that her life experience so far would enable her to pass this because she would be able to tick the boxes.

When you get your final interview, more about that in another chapter, or you're in force interview, or your senior interview (they get called different things.) That's when they're going to make a determination about your values, and your strengths, and whether you're the right person, the right fit for their force.

This bit here – the assessors don't even know which force you're replying to. All they know is your name, apparently. I think someone told me they know your email address as well which is a bit creepy, but never mind I'm sure they need to know that for some reason.

So what are we going to do to structure our approach over a five-minute period? Well, for many of you if you Google, 'how to answer interview questions,' you're going to find STAR.

Situation, Task, Action, and Result.

Or you might even find STARE: Situation, Task, Action, Result, and Evaluation.

The problem is though, these models are only used because they spell a word. A lot of people get really confused about the difference between a task and an action. 'Well, isn't one in the past and one's what I did? Oh, hang on a minute. One is what I intended to do and one's what I did. No hang on a minute, I'm not sure.'

And besides which, who talks like that? Who says things like, 'so the task I set myself,' or 'the task I was set...?'

No one talks like that. Not even in the police.

And the evaluate part, 'so I evaluated my performance....'

No, you didn't. No one talks like that, not even in the police.

If you ever said in the police how you'd evaluated something, you just have people pulling your leg and laughing at you, that just doesn't happen.

So what are we going to do instead? Well, over the years, over the quarter of a century that I've been coaching and supporting people for their interviews, I've come up with all sorts of different models. The one I've settled on for the past decade is something called SAARL, that's a bare minimum. Sometimes we add a KU to it, but more about that in the final interview, the senior interview chapter.

So, what does SAARL stand for?

Situation, Aim, Action, Result, Learning

Let's break this down further.

Situation.

So, you're going to talk about the specifics of the situation and you're also going to talk about the impact of that situation, the impact of that problem if you did nothing to deal with it. From there we're going to move into the Aim.

Aim

What is it that you aimed to achieve and then what options did you consider to get to that aim, and why did you choose the option that you chose?

Actions

So now we have an option that we've picked, what we need to do now is describe the Actions that we took. So, what you need to do here, and this is the bulk of your answer, is to describe not just what you did but how you did it.

Let me give you an example of some of the poor practice that people often display when I do my one-to-one coaching or in the webinars. And remember, it's not their fault because no one's told them or shown them how to answer an interview question. It's no fault of theirs. It's not something you're ever taught really at college or university or at school, with the odd exception. Most of my clients tell me no one's ever shown them how to answer interview questions. So, this is a key message - you're going to talk about what you did but then you're also going to talk about how you did it. It's the how you did it that is going to score you the points because it's the how, that often is what the behaviours within the value and competencies is looking for.

Let me give you an example of that. One of the exercises I often do on my interactive webinars is something called, 'The Seven Levels of How.' It's a little exercise I do to help them understand why the how is so important. I'll use it when clients say things like, 'so I spoke to the rest of my team and because of that, I knew that what they all wanted to do was to do x y and z.'

So, I'll say, 'so you spoke to your team. How did you do that?"

'Well, I held a meeting with them.'

'Great, you held a meeting. How did you do 'held a meeting?'

'Well, I explained to them what the problem was and then managed to find out from them what they thought about the problem.'

'Great, how did you do 'manage to find out?'

'Well, I...' and the penny often drops at this point. 'Well, I asked them questions.'

'Brilliant. How did you ask them questions?'

'Well, I asked them open questions.'

'Fantastic. How did you do 'asking them open questions?'

And that's when they'll say things like, 'so to get the information from the team, I knew I had to ask relevant open questions. So, the first thing I asked was what their thoughts were on the current situation. And then they told me what those thoughts were, and sometimes their answers were a bit vague so I followed them up with probing questions such as, what exactly do you mean by that or what do you feel the causes might be.'

See how we are getting right into the detail here? Even to the extent, especially on some of the courses I've run for serving police officers who want to get promoted to sergeant and inspector, we start talking about the difference between catalytic and cathartic questions.

Cathartic questions are questions like, 'so how did that make you feel?' You just want to know how people feel about something, catharsis. Catalytic questions are designed to be a catalyst to get information from people, such as, 'what do you think the possible causes would be in respect of this issue?' 'What do you believe the possible solutions might be?' Those are catalytic questions.

So that's just one example. What you did was you 'spoke to everyone,' I want to know how you did it. So, it's the how that's really important. Honestly, we spend hours on this in my webinars. On the final interview webinar, which is a two-hour webinar where we go through a trial run of the sort of interview that you're going to get, we probably spend the bulk of it, a good 45 minutes to an hour talking about that sort of detail. That's the level of granular detail in your answers that is required, because that's what's going to get you over the line in terms of a pass, a very good pass.

The same goes for the online assessment centre as well. You've got five minutes to talk. It's a long time. It is a long time to talk, and you need to fill it with point-scoring information that enables the assessor to score you highly.

This is not about… and I often see this in the Bluelight Facebook Group, where people ask for advice about interviews, and the advice is things like, 'just learn your competencies.' Or I've seen it in books elsewhere, 'learn phrases and words from the Competency Framework and just repeat those.'

No, that won't work in your online assessment centre. You need to describe how you've done things. Don't just make bold claims that you've done something. Describe how you did it.

And in your final interview, if you start trying to give the assessors, who will be serving police officers, serving senior officers who are out there on the front line now, if you start giving them that kind of 'BS,' those sort of phrases from the Competency and Values Framework, telling them what you think they want to hear, they will tune out from you straight away and they will fail you for it. I absolutely promise you. They'll fail you for using buzzwords.

You can't get through the process by using buzzwords. I don't care what anyone says in any other book or in any other guidance. I've been that interviewer. I've been coaching and supporting people for police recruitment, police specialist interviews, police promotion boards for over 25 years now. I know this having been in the interviewer's hot seat because I used to be one of the interviewers. I know that when candidates start coming out with buzzwords and phrases from an assessment framework or a competency framework, I just tune out. Or I may just be a little bit sneaky and say, 'so you worked collaboratively with the rest of your team, how exactly did you do that?' And whatever buzz word they come up with. whenever they come up with a buzzword, I'll go back and say, 'so previously you said, 'the buzzword phrase.' What do you mean by that? How did you do that buzzword."

It's because I'm a bit annoyed with them, to be frank. So don't do it. Just don't go there. Describe how you did things. It's great to say what you did but then follow up with how you did it. Now if it sounds to you like I'm really emphasising this, it's because it's so, so important. It is one of the biggest traps that people fall into. It's the same on application forms as well. People describing lots of bold claims of what they did but no 'how' behind it. No substance. And remember, the police are obsessed by evidence, so they want to see evidence that you are demonstrating the skills that they're looking for.

That's going to become relevant in a moment because what I'm going to do with you, I'm going to share some questions with you from one of my question banks.

I provide those clients of mine who are preparing for the online assessment centre with a question bank of possible questions they're going to get. So far, the feedback has been awesome, so I know I'm on the right lines. Similarly for the final interview as well. I'll give you some more examples in the chapters that look at the final / senior force interview.

So let's look at some examples for you.

First, from the value of Transparency. The question would be:
'Please can you tell me about a time when you've had to make a difficult decision where you had to account for your decision to others.'

Another possibility would be:

'Please can you tell me about a time when you've made a difficult decision where others may not have agreed with you. How did you manage the disagreement?'

Now you might be thinking, they sound a bit similar. Well, it's because it's the same question, it's just worded differently. So always be prepared for a variation on a theme. But always answer the question. Always answer the question. Now in my of guidance I also provide supplementary points.

So these supplementary points will be what the marking guide from the College of Policing is based on. The supplementary points I've come up with for you are based on the behaviours, which are described in the Competency and Values Framework. But what I've done is I've turned the behavioural statements into something that makes more sense and is easier to read.

So, the supplementary points for this question would be: '

'What rationale did you use for your decision-making?

'What information did you get from people?'

'Where did you get that information from?'

'How did you choose those individuals to get the information?'

'How did you get the information from them?'

'How did you weigh up the pros and cons of that information?'

'How did you analyse it?'

'How did you actually come up with the rationale for your decision?'

'How did you ensure that your decision was the right one to make?'

So, this last point would be as simple as in your decision-making process, perhaps going to someone like a mentor or someone who you trust in the workplace, or even your boss and say, 'Look I've got this difficult decision. I'm not quite sure what to do and I'm quite sure it's something that you've faced in the past. How would you deal with this?' Or, 'this is how I'm proposing that I deal with it. What do you think?' So, you're getting advice from someone else, and this enables you to ensure that your decision was the right one to make.

How did you ensure that others understood your decision-making rationale? This is why they've asked you the question, where you've had to account for others or where others may not have agreed with you, how did you manage the disagreement? So, I want to hear about how you explained your decision-making process to other people who may not have agreed with you.

And then the last supplementary point is:

'How did you manage any feedback following your decision?'

So, this may have been people who've given you advice to say, 'do you know, one of the things that might work better would be...' Feedback is a gift. I know it sounds like a cliché, but it's a gift you can choose to accept that or choose not to.

It's difficult at times to accept feedback from people, especially if it's critical or when they say, 'I'm going to give you some constructive criticism.' I hate that phrase, by the way. Because it's got the word 'criticism' in it. If someone's going to be constructive then they're going to give me some feedback. They're going to share with me their thoughts, and they're going to do it in a very supportive way. But if they're going to give you 'constructive criticism?' I used to say, 'actually, no thanks, I don't want any criticism. If you want to give me some feedback that's going to be helpful, then great let's do it, but I don't want to be criticized.' Who wants to be criticized? Especially when you've been bold enough to make a decision.

Remember there's only one thing worse than a poor decision. That's no decision at all. So as a police officer you've got to be a decision-maker.

So, let's do another one. Hopefully, that last one makes sense to you. Let's do another one from the same question bank I put together for the Online Assessment Centre. This is for the competency of, We take Ownership.

So, the question might be something like:

'Please can you tell me about a time when you've taken responsibility for a task'

or it could also be:

'Please can you tell me about a time when you have worked with others to manage a task'

Equally, it could be phrased as:

'Please can you tell me about a time when you've taken responsibility for solving a problem.'

Or it could be:

'Please can you tell about a time when you've taken responsibility, or you've worked with others to solve a problem.'

So, expect any variation on the theme for those questions.

Supplementary points:

'How did you identify the problem?'

So, you could think about how urgent it was or its importance, and how the problem emerged, and then how did you seek the views and feedback on the problem from others.

So this is a similar sort of process that you're following in the decision-making. You're getting information from other people to enable you to come up with the best way forward.

'How did you go about helping others involved in the problem-solving?'

This is about you being a helpful leader and supporting and enabling other people.

'How did you get others to help or support you in the problem-solving?'

You needed support and help as well. How did you get other people to get involved in the problem?

'How did you react to any mistakes made or when things did not go to plan?'

This is important in any interview, because I don't want candidates trying to persuade me that everything they touch turns to gold and everything in the garden is always rosy. Because in the policing world, it isn't. Mistakes are always being made. I made mistakes daily. They weren't mistakes at the time, they were the best decisions I could make with the information I had access to at that time. But it later turned out that what I thought was happening wasn't the case and, I made a mistake. But how I rectified that is more important than just realising, 'oh, no. I've made a mistake. I know, I'll do nothing.' What you should be thinking is, 'right, what do I need to do about it to put the wheel back on, to make sure I don't make that mistake again?'

And then the last part which would be the icing on the cake:

'How did you identify your strengths and areas for development?'

Think about what you did to address these? What is it you'd do better next time? And that kind of links in nicely, it's a perfect link to the last part of the SAARL process where you will talk about the Result. So, what was the result? And like I said, don't try and persuade people that everything that you touch turns to gold and everything is perfect that you deal with because that's not how the world works.

Result

The assessor, especially when it comes to the final interview (I'll cover this part of the process in more detail in another chapter), would probably be thinking, 'well that wasn't challenging enough because it all worked out perfectly or it's something that they just do daily. They're just doing their job.' In an interview answer I want to hear about something that was challenging and difficult for you. If it was challenging and difficult then things didn't go to plan. You can describe how things didn't go to plan and as an interviewer I'd love to hear about that.

Because what you can do after that is you can talk about the Learning that came from it.

Learning

The learning phase isn't things like, 'I learned the power of open questions,' or 'I learned it's good to talk to people'. Those are just statements of fact.

I want to know what comes after this phrase (which you can use in your interview), 'so if I had my time again, with the same set of circumstances, what I would do differently is......' That's what I want to hear. What would you do differently? But in granular detail - the learning based on that specific set of circumstances.

Now that should be enough to get you started in your preparation for the Stage 2. In the Final interview chapter, I'll also cover the K and U which stands for knowledge and understanding. But for this process here, for this five-minute answer, I think that's probably enough.

So hopefully all of that makes sense in terms of the sort of questions you're going to get, how you would structure your answers, and what possible questions you could get asked. I've just given you a bit of a flavour really of the types of questions that you could get asked and how you'd get marked by the assessor using the supplementary points.

Now, one of the big questions I always get in my webinars is, 'can I use notes that I've prepared before each stage of the assessment?'

Well, the College of Policing guidance is really clear. You cannot use notes that you've pre-prepared before the Stage 2 exercise. The same goes for Stage 3. The same for the Situational Judgment Test. That is their guidance. That is their rule, that is their policy. You can't use notes that you have used or put together before the actual assessment starts.

The thing is you are being recorded. What they can see in front of you is being recorded. What the camera can see is being recorded. So, what I'd say there is that you can make notes during the exercise. The guidance makes it clear that you can make notes during the 1-minute preparation phase, before your five-minute answer. You can make notes in the Stage 3 as well. You can make notes all the way through the Stage 3 Written exercise, and there's no camera on you anyway in the written exercise. And then the Stage 3 Briefing, you can make notes in the 10-minute briefing phase and then the 1-minute before each one of the answers. I'll come to that in more detail in the Stage 3.

So all I would say is you can make notes but what you choose to make notes on is up to you. You can make notes during the exercise, during that 1-minute preparation phase or the 10 minutes if it's a Stage 3 briefing, but what you choose to make notes on is up to you. It's your decision. That's all I'll say. I'll just park that there for you. However, I'll say it again, the College of Policing guidance is clear. You can't use notes that you've pre-prepared before the assessment centre, before the assessment, and before each stage of that assessment.

So folks, there you go. Hopefully that chapter has been helpful for you, to guide you and steer you through the foundations of what you need to do to ensure that you score really, really well in the Stage 2. And if you're thinking it's impossible to score 100%. No, it isn't. Several of my clients recently have scored 100% in their Stage 2 interview.

HOW TO SUCCEED IN THE POLICE RECRUITMENT PROCESS

These are individuals who've attended my webinars. We've worked hard with each other. I've really pushed them, and pushed them, and pushed them to deliver excellence in their answers. Eventually, when we've got to the point where they've delivered those excellent answers in our practice sessions, oh my goodness they've been awesome. They've gone away and got 100%, but they put the time and effort into achieving that score. So, they've done the hard work. I've shown them the way and they've done the hard work. So hopefully, what I've shown you in this chapter will give you the incentive to start working hard so that you're going to get one of those high marks as well.

And why is it so important that you get a high mark as opposed to just a pass? Well, I think I've mentioned it before, how forces can be choosy? Some of them are just looking for a pass because they need the numbers, like the Metropolitan Police, who have hundreds of officers in every intake. Other forces, especially the 'Shire' forces, who may only have 1200 or up to 2000 officers in their force, they don't need hundreds. They just need an intake of 25. Maybe two intakes of 25 once a year. That's all they need. 50 officers every year. That's all they can afford and that's all they need. But they will still get thousands applying.

The only way that forces can whittle the numbers down is based on the score. So, if 200 people pass the Online Assessment Centre and they've only got the capability to run 100 interviews for 50 vacancies, they've got to cut down that 200 to 100. And it's not about the amount of time they've got. It's also about the resources they have because people have got to conduct those interviews. Some forces may just not have the resources to run 200 interviews. So, they will have to reduce that 200 down to 100. The only legitimate way they can do that, and this is based on case law as well, I'm not going to go into the detail of the case law, but the only legitimate way they can do that is by utilising your score at your assessment centre. That's why it's so important that you strive all the time to score the best score that you possibly can, aiming for 100% You're not just aiming for a pass.

I sometimes see this in the Bluelight Police Recruitment Facebook Group, where I see people comment, 'I passed and only spoke for two and a half minutes.' I wouldn't be so proud of that. What I'd be proud of is the fact that I spoke for 5 minutes. I gave a really detailed answer that was incredibly well structured. That hit all the behaviours that they were looking for and I got 100% - that's something to be proud of. And that person is pretty much guaranteed they're going to go through to the next phase.

So one of my clients, recently Dave, Dave C. I'm not going to embarrass him by using his surname. He got a phone call from the recruiting team for the force he was applying to, after he told was told by email he got a pass at the assessment centre. He got a phone call to congratulate him because he got the highest score they've ever seen. He's so proud of that achievement. He's now got offers from three forces, three forces! Incredible. But it's because he's done that hard work.

I know I keep emphasising this and I know it might sound like a broken record, but success won't happen by osmosis. There is no magic bullet. I will show you the way, but you've got to do the hard work. If you do that hard work, if you do what I ask you to do, and you keep doing it obsessively then you will pass. I guarantee it.

I do that for my courses, I guarantee that you'll pass. If you don't pass and you've done the work I've asked you to do, you get a refund. I mean how simple and how fair is that? How fair can I be? I'm all in on this journey. Are you all in as well?

I know I'm going to mention this again and again and again but it's so important. You might only get one crack at this. I sometimes hear people say, 'well I'll give it a go this time and if I don't pass, I'll try again in six months' time.' Why waste your time? Prepare to pass now and prepare to excel in everything you do. If you carry that attitude through your policing career, I promise you you're going to do well. Anyway, I'm going off a completely different tangent now.

Chapter 11 - The Online Assessment Centre Stage 3 Written Exercise

In this chapter, we're going to look at the Stage 3 of the Online Assessment Centre. I'm going to break into two parts because the stage 3 is broken into two parts. The first part is a written exercise, and the second part is on what we call a briefing exercise. It's not quite a briefing, but I'll explain more about that in the next chapter.

By the end of this chapter, you should have a really good idea about the structured approach that you're going to utilise in the written exercise.

First of all, a little bit about the written exercise and the practicalities of it. Depending on the guidance that you've been given by the College of Policing, it will probably tell you that you've got 40 minutes to do this exercise. However, you haven't. You've got 2 hours to do it in. You've got up to 2 hours. I think what the College of Policing meant was they expect it'll take you 40 minutes but they're giving you 2 hours to do it in. So, when it says you've got 40 minutes to complete this exercise, if you've got that version of the guidance, ignore it. You've got 2 hours.

I've coached and supported hundreds, probably over a thousand people through this process now. Easily over a thousand and not one of them has come back to me to say, 'no, Brendan, it's actually 40 minutes.' It really is 2 hours. That should relax your nerves a little bit because that's plenty of time. Although, my clients, especially the ones that go on my webinars, tell me that they spent all the time, just typing away, typing away, utilising every moment of that 2 hours because they'd got so much to write about.

What else can I tell you about? Oh, yes. The College of Policing guidance also says that you don't need to have any police knowledge or experience to be able to undertake Stage 3. That might be right, that might be true if you're just looking for a basic pass. However, hundreds of people in the Facebook group who I've done a survey with, when I asked them the question, 'is this is correct?' came back and said, 'no, it's not.' They explained how it's really advantageous to have some policing experience under your belt, especially if you want to score a really high mark.

What we're looking for here is for you to get a mark that's 90% plus in your stage 3, and that is possible. So many of my clients come back and tell me that they've scored 90% plus. 96% is the highest mark I've seen, 96%!! This individual completely smashed it, completely aced it. How did he do it? He just followed the template that we worked on in the webinars. But you're not here on the webinar now. You're reading it as one of the chapters in your book. Whichever way, you are going to get a good grounding.

What else can I tell you about the practicalities? There's no camera on you. Unlike the other exercises, the Stage 3 Briefing and the Stage 2 interview, there is no camera on you for this process. And don't buy anything that your force tells you that you might get one of the assessors from the College of Policing checking on you. No, they won't, and no, they haven't. That has not happened once. There's not some secret bank of ninja assessors in some bunker in the College of Policing headquarters waiting around at 3 o'clock in the morning because you could do this anytime you want. 24/7, you can do it at any time in the one-week window you get given. There's no one there. There's no one at the other end. You're just submitting this onto the template they give you, answering the questions that they ask you. And to reiterate, there's no camera on you.

The College of Policing also says that you can't use notes that you've pre-prepared before. I want to make sure that you follow that guidance. However, there's no camera on you and what you choose to make notes on is your business because you can make notes during the exercise itself. What you choose to make notes on is your business. There's no camera on you. I'll just leave that there for you.

What are they going to give you? Well, they're going to give you some kind of community policing scenario. They're going to put you in a position of a constable in an area that is suffering from, my guess it's got something to do with young people. Some form of antisocial behaviour at a certain location where they congregate, and members of the community are getting really annoyed by it, and especially about the lack of police action. They may give you some figures to confuse you that show that reports of anti-social behaviour and crime are going down, but that should just tell you that, yes, reports are going down, but does that mean that the number of incidents is going down? Does it mean that reports are going down because people aren't reporting those incidents anymore, because they've lost faith in the police?

They're going to give you a little package of information. It's probably going to take about 10 to 15 minutes to work through it and then you need to have a structured approach to answer their questions. If you've got a structured approach to this issue, it doesn't really matter if they change the scenario. In a couple of months, they could change it to something else, it doesn't matter. If you've got the structured approach that I'm going to tell you about now, you'll be able to nail it every day of the week.

How can I say this with confidence? Well, I spent 28 years in the police service. Not all of it was in Community Policing but just under 8 years was, where I spent those years as a community police inspector, a neighbourhood inspector, in two different areas. The approach I took to problem solving and community engagement was unique at the time. This was over fifteen years ago, but the approach was incredibly unique. Why? Because the involvement of citizens was way beyond what any of the other neighbourhood teams had. I remember Sir Robert Peel, he was the founder of Police Service in 1829, when he founded Metropolitan Police, he talked about how the:

'Police are the public and the public are the police. The police just being members of the public who are paid full-time to carry out a role which is incumbent on all citizens in the interest of community welfare and existence.'

I looked at that and thought, 'so, what most Neighbourhood Teams are doing now is a sort of, 'You Said - We Did' approach. You tell us what the problems are, and we'll go away and address them, and then we'll come back to you and tell you what we've taken.

But that approach didn't seem to involve that much community / citizen-led action. It just seemed to lead to a very passive client-dependent relationship that we had with the community. And so, I developed what I thought were unique methods of community engagement and problem solving. Actually, there were one or two individuals in other parts of the country who were developing a similar approach, and I got to meet them later in my career. But for several years, I pioneered an approach which had, at its roots, a theory called Asset-Based Community Development. This was where I enabled members of the community to take their own action to resolve problems in their communities.

I'm not talking about them patrolling the streets. I'm not talking about anything like that. I'm talking about what they could do to ensure that their community was the best version of itself it could be, and they had responsibility for that. It's not my job. It's not a police officer's job or the council's job to create a community that's the best version of itself it can be. It's only citizens within that community that can do that.

The approach I pioneered was less, 'You Said, We Did,' and more, 'You Said, and We Said, How can I enable and support you to create the best version of this community that can be?' It's very much a forward-looking process and is very much about creating a positive vision for the future.

At the same time however, we the police, we had an important job to do, in terms of enforcement, tackling organised criminality, dealing with the drug dealers, the loan sharks, the people who were running modern-day slavery rackets. We had a lot on our plate but at the same time, what we recognised was, if we remove all those illegitimate leaders within the community, and they are dealt with either by imprisonment or by other means, or they reconcile themselves and start seeing the light and become useful citizens again, and that happened, that did sometimes happen. We offered support to everyone we arrested, to enable them to find a path that will take them away from a criminal lifestyle. Anyway, back to the point, the enforcement, and the removal of the illegitimate leadership - what that leads is a vacuum, a space in the community, and if you don't fill that vacuum with strong cohesive community, it'll just get filled by more criminals who do the same thing as the ones you have just removed. And then you'll end up doing the same thing all over again, and it's not really doing anything to enable that community to improve itself.

So, the approach we're going to take in our Stage 3 is very much an Asset-Based one where we're going to enable the citizens in the community. That goes back to Sir Robert Peel's, one of his original principles that I've just mentioned, because he talked about the police just being members of the public. They're just paid to carry out a role, which is incumbent on every citizen. He didn't say, though, in the interest of catching the bad guys. He didn't say in the interest of community safety. He didn't say in the interest of reducing crime. What he said was in the interest of, 'community welfare and existence.' That's the approach I took. What can we do to enable this community to be the strongest version of itself? One where young people have got hope and promise? One where it's got a strong sense of, 'community welfare and existence.'

You might be thinking, 'wow, this just sounds really good but is it based on any research?' Well, actually, it is. Later in my career, I got to work in the Strategic Change Branch in Greater Manchester Police, where my job was to improve the problem-solving capability of the force at a street level, at a neighbourhood level. How do you get to do that? Well, I didn't succeed. It would take me 20 years and a whole army of advisors and people who can guide and support to enable that to happen. But we nudged away, and we started off a process, we acted as a catalyst for many neighbourhoods who did start taking this kind of approach. It was really pleasing to see how they got remarkable results because of it.

From there, I ended up working as a consultant to forces, to the College of Policing and spent 3 years on the International Advisory Board of a European project that was looking to improve community engagement and problem-solving across Europe, mainly in Central Europe and Eastern Europe.

I also got to speak at conferences in this country, in Budapest in Hungary and in Munich, Germany, at their Police College. A lot of involvement, post retirement, in community policing methods, community engagement methods. What I'm presenting to you here is a very shortened foundation version of something that I could talk to you about for hours and hours and hours on end. But we haven't got that kind of time in this book, and certainly, if I did go into great depths, the chapter itself would, indeed, become a book. So, I hope this reassurance will suffice, that everything I'm going to talk to you about is based on solid, solid research.

What sort of questions they're going to ask you? Actually, let's wind back. Just to remind you, I think the scenario is going to be based on antisocial behaviour. Probably young people, it's going to be a certain location, it's going to be a community that's sick of reporting things, but nothing ever gets done, a very basic type of problem like that.

You're addressing your answers to your sergeant, by the way. So, your sergeant is giving you a scenario and your sergeant is asking you some questions for you to answer, and I think they're going to be questions along these lines:

Can you please describe the problem as you see it?

How do you see your role in the problem-solving process?

What are potential causes of this behaviour?

What would you like to do initially?

What potential impact is this problem going to have on the community if nothing is done about it?

Which organisations are you going to work with and why?

What solutions would you propose?

How are you going to improve community relations?

How are you going to assess and monitor your progress?

I don't know if these are the questions, but these are the types of questions that they can ask you because these questions are based on a problem-solving methodology which is called SARA, which stands for Scanning, Analysis, Response, and Assessment.

If you look up 'police problem solving,' in your preferred search engine it will bring up the SARA model. I'm not going to go into the SARA model in any great depth, other than to describe how we've broken it down into different stages for you, using an advanced community engagement methodology that incorporates the guidance and the research from the SARA model. But you can look it up yourself. There's plenty of research out there that's open source. Like I said, just put in something like 'problem-oriented policing,' 'SARA,' 'police problem-solving.' If you search that sort of thing, it will bring up loads and loads of information for you. Enough bedtime reading for several weeks.

Anyway, back to the actual exercise itself. If those are the questions, you need a structured approach to be able to deal with the community problem.

Step 1

Describe the Headline Problem

The first thing we're going to do is we're going to describe the headline problem. The way we're going to do this is we're going to use our five WH's. We're going to ask questions of the problem. Questions like, when is it occurring? Where exactly is it occurring? Who is it that's involved? Those sorts of questions. We're going to use our full range of five WH questions to be able to describe the problem in as much rich detail as we possibly can.

Now, there may also be some little traps for you in the exercise where they give you vague information. They may say something like there's up to 30 young people, but that's a trap. It's not 30 young people, it's up to 30 young people, which means that you don't have the right information.

The exercise may say how the problems are occurring in the evenings. What does that mean? That could be 5 o'clock to 11 o'clock. That could be 4 o'clock until midnight. It could be 7 o'clock until 9 o'clock. It's open to interpretation. It's absolutely meaningless until you start defining it. Does that make sense so far? So, you also need to talk about the information that's not there, as well as the information that is there when describing the headline problem.

Step 2

Gathering Information and Intelligence

From there, we're going to start looking at the information and intelligence that we have, that's going to help us understand the problem. Also, what information and intelligence are missing, and where we would get it from. This is where you're going to start thinking about all the different stakeholders that you're going to be working with. If it's young people, I'd be working with social services, youth services, the council, education sector, mental health team, drug and alcohol action teams, and depending on what the problem is, environmental services and licensing if it's drink-related antisocial behaviour. We're putting together all the different organisations who are going to be capable of giving you the information that you need. Because unless you got information from all those different agencies about the problem, you're not going to be capable of doing some good analysis. Bear in mind, all of this is work that you need to do before you start implementing any solutions.

Step 3

Form a Working Group

The next stage after this is how you're going to form a working group from of all the people who've got a stake in the issue. You're working group is also going to involve members of the community. If you've got a local councillor, get them involved. If you've got shopkeepers who are annoyed about everything that's going on or the lack of police action, get the shopkeepers involved. If you've got very vocal members of the community, bring them into your working group. Remember what Sir Robert Peel said, he talked about police officers just being members of the public who are paid full-time to carry out a role which is incumbent on all citizens in the interest of community welfare and existence. This is why others should be involved.

Step 4

Asset Mapping

Now, we've got our working group together, we want to expand it. The way we're going to do that is we are going to do some asset mapping in the community. This is also how we're going to develop our community relationships. We're going to look for people in the community who are capable, connected, care enough to act, and who are committed to act – I call this the '4Cs.' The assets within the community, these are the people in the community who are already doing awesome things. They might not be in a formal role like a home watch coordinator, but they might be the woman or the man on the road that seems to know everyone else in the road and is the go-to person if there's any problems. Or someone who runs a kickabout on a Saturday morning with a group of young people, playing football on the field. Could we help them expand on that? Could we enable them to develop the kickabout into a formal team to represent the community? The assets are already involved in the community, but not always in a formal way, but they'll be delighted to get involved in a group that's looking at creating the best version of that community that it could possibly be.

So now, we've got all these assets in the community - actually, there's a lot more to developing this. In the webinars, we talk about how exactly we would undergo a process of asset mapping all the way to membership of your working group. There are many pitfalls, as by doing this you will come across issues in the community that have been, so far, unresolved. You could destroy community confidence, very quickly, with your asset mapping process, unless you've got certain measures in place.

Step 5

Problem Analysis

So, you're going to get all those assets into your working group. In reality, this takes months, but in your exercise, it's going to take, I don't know, days. Then we're going to do some problem analysis with members of the community. We're going to look at things like the problem analysis triangle, where we look at the causes and the impact, from a victim's perspective, offender's perspective, and the location. We're also going to look at all the individuals who we are targeting, the young people who are causing antisocial behaviour. Are they offenders, perpetrators, or are they victims of circumstance?

So, you might want to look at research around things like Adverse Childhood Experiences - this is where you start looking at not just the causes, but the causes of the causes. If the cause of their behaviour is boredom and a lack of parental control, what's the cause of that? What is the cause of that? The cause of the lack of parental control could be one of the many things that are listed in the research around Adverse Childhood Experiences. That's another offshoot of something that I'd like you to research. I could talk for hours about Adverse Childhood Experiences, but I'm not going to. For the moment, I'm just going to point you in the right direction.

Step 6

Creating a Vision for the Community

Where are we up to now? We've done our problem analysis. Now, we're able to start setting a vision for that community as opposed to asking the community to tell us what the problems are. Why? Because as soon as we ask what the problems are, members of the community are going to tell us what they are and expect us to go and solve those problems. It's quite a reasonable thing, really, isn't it? If you ask members of the community, 'tell us all about your problems and priorities,' and a lot of forces do this, it's not an unreasonable expectation that members of the community will tell you all about their problems and priorities.

Then there's an expectation, a reasonable expectation that you're going to do something about it. What tends to happen is they tell you about really complex social problems that can't be resolved overnight, or even be resolved over a month. You could go back to them after a month and say, 'the problem still exists.' But that could reduce community confidence because they just think, 'well, yeah. What are you doing? You said you'd solve all these problems, and you haven't.'

So, we're going to take a different approach. We are going to ask the community to create a vision of the best version of the community it could be through questions like:

'In 2 or 3 years, if you had all the resources you needed, and all the money you needed, what would the best version of this community look and feel like if we could build on all the good things that exist already?'

Once they start describing what this would be we can get them to draw it – this is something that is called Rich Picturing. It comes from the soft systems approach to problem-solving and it's something I've done a lot of, and it really helps people, to galvanize groups of people together to get the shared vision of what a community could look like.

Now, they've created a strong concrete and compelling vision for their community, the next question isn't about, 'so, is the council and police will go away and deal with this?'

No, it's not. That's the worst thing you could do.

Step 7

Co-Creating Solutions

What we're going to do now is we're going to lay the foundation for a set of challenging questions for the community.

'That's your vision of your community, where young people are doing more positive things in that community, they're engaged in sport, they're engaged in clubs, they're helping to support people who are elderly, elderly people are helping them through their lives, and it's this great connected community that has loads of activities in it. But it's not for the police to create that. It's not for the police to run the football clubs, the boxing clubs. It's not their role to do that. You, the community are more than capable of doing all these things.'

Now we are going to ask them:

'If that's your vision, what steps do you need to take to get to that vision?

What things do you need to do?

What solutions do you need to put in place now and in the future, to enable that to happen?'

The community members will describe what steps are needed. Then the next set of questions from the police are:

'How can I support you?

How can we, the police and council support you to do those things?'

The ideas that come from members of the community, in reality, from the work I've done, are things like football clubs, walking clubs, a support group for people who are care leavers, a support group for people who have only recently left prison, and have got no support from family. All sorts of groups that help connect the community and enable it to be a better place.

All these individual groups, we're going to bring them together in what will be like a team of teams. They might be a football team, it could be a cheerleading squad, it doesn't really matter what it is. They're all doing things to bring people in the community together and we're the ones that are going to enable them to come together in a 'team of teams' or an 'association of associations.' I hope you're still with me on this because now we've got a massive working group because this is now our working group, the association of the associations is our working group. It's grown, and grown, and grown.

The last one I ran ended up having over 50 people in it, representing over 42 different community groups. The other people were members of their council and local councillors, and people in the housing association. It was a massive community group that started with just two people, me, and my colleague from the Council.

What are we going to do for this group? We're going to enable them to do the things that they're perfectly capable of doing, and this will help develop a really strong community. The people who were the initial complainers are probably going to be in your working group and this is how we improve community relationships. This is how we look at helping others to create solutions. Everything I've just talked about just now, although based in the reality of my policing experience, will also help answer all the questions that you're probably going to get at your Stage 3 written.

I'm just looking at the size of this chapter now. I could talk for hours about this subject.

But in our answers, we're also going not just talk about what the community is going to do, there's a role for the police as well. What I am going to explain next is a model which you won't find in any research. It's what I put together as a neighbourhood inspector years ago.

So, when we decided to do any kind of enforcement, we also 'TEPAC' it. What does TEPAC stand for?

Trust-building – Carry out activities to ensure the community members see the police as the legitimate agents of law and order

Enforcement - We're going to undertake actions to prevent the problem in the first place. Otherwise, we'll be enforcing it week in, week out.

Prevention – We're going to carry out activities with partner organisations to prevent the crime or ASB happening again.

Advocacy - We're going to act as advocates for the community through the provision of resources and funding.

Communication - communicate, communicate. We're going to get members of the public to do a lot of communicating, about what we're doing. How? By inviting members of the public on ride-alongs, getting to them come and watch the warrants we execute, get them to come and see what we're doing on Friday nights to tackle the night-time economy problems.

TEPAC stands for Trust-building, Enforcement, Prevention, Advocacy, and Communication.

There is a role for the police in all of this, but the police role tends to be around the enforcement that's needed. We look at a lot of things like this on the webinars. Honestly, we spend about 4 hours on this and all I've got here in this chapter is about 20 minutes' worth.

I could talk for far more than four hours about it, but I'm not going to. I've just not got the time and your book is going to be huge if I start sharing everything that I know about problem-solving in communities, and the scenarios that they're going to give you. Actually, this chapter would become a book in its own right!

Step 8

Monitor, Assess and Support

All we're going to do now is we're going to monitor, assess, and support those community groups, which leaves us free to take any necessary enforcement action.

Remember, when we get young people into the criminal pathway, we don't have to have send them to court. We can use alternative methods to help support them. Durham Constabulary does this very well. They've got something called, 'Checkpoint.' So, you might want to look that up. I give all my clients this huge list of resources, which they can look at to get ideas, innovative ideas that they can use in their Stage 3.

This, by the way, is how to get 90% plus at this stage. We form a template in the webinars of how to deal with the written exercise in a way that it's going to give you 90% plus. That's what the webinars are. That's why I think they're so amazing. They so, so work because in the space of 2 hours, a 2-hour webinar, we work through one of the scenarios that's probably very similar to the one that you're going to get. That enables the clients on that webinar to use the work we do during those 2 hours, as a template.

This is what gives them a score of 90% plus in their Stage 3.
They don't need to have any police experience because they're using me vicariously. They're using my experience in problem-solving. Like I said, it's far more advanced than what you're going to see in most forces because I've been developing these techniques over about 15 years.

As I said earlier, they're not just Brendan's techniques. They're based on sound and solid research, as to what works in the police in this country and other countries in the European Union, across the water in United States, and in associated areas like the health service and education. We've looked at what works in community building as well, in community organising. Barack Obama, he was a community organiser before he became a politician. All the principles around asset-based community development, we incorporate those into our problem-solving process.

If you'd like to discover more about the research I refer to, go to the website for an organisation called Intensive Engagement at https://www.intensiveengagement.com

I know, what we have covered sounds like lots of buzz words, but it works. The bottom line is, if you follow the template, it will work. That's why I'm going to encourage you to attend the webinars if you possibly can, please do attend them. Join us on the webinars and then we can go into this in far more detail, far more detail than we've got the time to do in this book.

So, folks, I hope this has made sense to you. You're probably going to have to read this a few times. You're probably going to have to start thinking about real-life community problems for it to start making sense, but it will, it will make sense.

If you're on my online course now, if you decided to join, watch all the videos, look at the templates I provide and join me on the webinars where we work on real-life community problems like the ones you're going to get. This will enable you to get 90% plus.

Importantly, once you're in the police, you're going to find these techniques useful. So many of my clients come back to me and say that they're still using a lot of the techniques that we discussed, and they learned about during my courses in their policing career, and it's enabling them to be really, successful. That's just awesome to hear. It's just awesome to hear.

I hear from so many of my clients, over the years, especially when they're coming up to the next stage in their career, like promotion or going for a specialist interview. It's just great to hear from them and it's super great to also hear that they've utilised a lot of the methods that we discussed in their real-life policing career. But before you get to that point, you've got to jump through these hoops. Your Online Assessment Centre, Stage 3 Written, is one of those hoops. It can be quite a challenging one if you don't have that sort of familiarity with community policing that you should have, that you need to have, despite what the College of Policing says.

So, folks, I'm going to end on that. I hope you've enjoyed this chapter on the Stage 3 Written. In the next chapter, we're going to look at Stage 3 Briefing. Same models but we're going to apply it to a world of organised criminality, violent criminals, drug dealing, vulnerable people, and people who are homeless. You might be thinking, 'wow, that's a lot for me to deal with.'

Yeah, but that's what the College of Police are going to give you in the Briefing, and you've got 36 minutes to talk about it. That's a long time. You need to have something to talk about. In the next chapter, I'm going to tell you about the things that you can talk about to fill those 36 minutes, full of point-scoring material.

https://bluelightonline.co.uk/book

Chapter 12 - The Online Assessment Centre Stage 3 Briefing Exercise

This chapter - The final part of the Online Assessment Centre, is all about the Stage 3 Briefing.

Now, this is one that causes a lot of concern among the Bluelight Police Recruitment Facebook Group (are you a member yet? See the Offer Wall for details of how to join almost 20,000 members). Thousands of people have said how this is the one that they have found the most challenging. The reason why they find it really challenging is that this is where you're going to have to talk for 36 minutes about community policing and a conundrum that they're going to present you with. They're going to ask you 12 questions and you must deliver 12 x 3-minute answers.

The actual physical makeup of this assessment starts with 10 minutes where you get the opportunity to read a scenario. The scenario is probably going to be some quite vague paragraphs, I'm told that they're quite vague. Six or seven quite vague paragraphs are going to put you in a position where you're a constable in charge of a community that is being impacted by drug dealers, who often turn to violence. Those individuals who are taking the drugs are often homeless or vulnerable and the community is starting to suffer because of this.

You've got ten minutes to read those paragraphs. Ten minutes to make notes. You're on camera for this. Like I said before, you are allowed to make notes during the exercise. You can't use notes that you pre-prepared before, but what you choose to make notes on is your business.

After the 10-minute scenario you've been presented with, you are then expected to give a briefing, but the briefing is 12 questions that you're going to be asked about that scenario. You don't know what those questions are right at the very beginning because they just feed them in for you one at a time. You'll be given the first question and then you've got one minute to think about it. Then three minutes to answer it.

Now, I run a two-and-a-half-hour webinar on this where I put my clients into a position where I give them a scenario. Then I ask them the questions and give them three minutes to answer the questions. Trust me. Three minutes is a long time to talk if you're not prepared and if you're not knowledgeable and if you've not got an understanding of how to deal with some of these issues.

Fortunately, I do know how to deal with a lot of these issues. It's almost as if the Stage 3 was written for me. I've got a lot of experience in tackling organised criminality. A lot of experience dealing with people who are homeless and vulnerable. A lot of experience in community building – this is the one thing that needs to go with all of that. There's no point in tackling organised criminality and leaving a vacuum behind only to be filled by more organised criminality.

We need to fill that vacuum with a strong cohesive community. We're going to use a very similar model to answer the questions to what we used in our written exercise. We're going to think about the different stakeholders that we're going to work with. We're going to think about growing our working group. We're going to think about what intelligence and information they can bring to the group. How we're going to enable those individuals to join the working group and get involved? Not just people from the council and education and health. Not just people from the statutory sector but also people from the third sector, from the volunteer sector. People who have just got great ideas in the community.

Remember our Four C's - people who are Capable, Connected, they Care enough to act, and they're Committed to act as well. Because they give you quite a vague scenario, what I've done on my online course and for my webinars is I've given you a very specific scenario. I use a town in North Wales as a case study. I'm sorry, Wrexham, but I'm using you. I use Wrexham as an example scenario to provide the detail for you.

It's a great thing really that they give you a vague set of information and ask you to talk about it for 36 minutes. Because what that means is that you can add some specific detail into those three-minute chunks. And you're going to be right. You're going to score really highly. Remember how the people who follow my template are the people who are scoring 90% plus in their Stage 3.

We start off by using Wrexham as a scenario, with lots of newspaper articles, clips of newspaper articles, clips of videos, and storyline to go with it. You can then actually hang your hat on something. For the 10-minute Briefing scenario, a lot of my clients just think of it as Wrexham.

Now, I did a little bit of work a few years ago with Wrexham Police and Wrexham Council. I've got a good insight into some of the problems that they are dealing with and they're very, very complex, hugely complex social problems that they are having to tackle here. Certainly, the police don't have all the answers and don't have all the solutions. As with any area that is suffering from the sort of issues, they're not going to be ones that are going to be cured overnight. So, this is why I use Wrexham as a case study.

The first set of questions are going to probably be things like the below. These are some of the example questions we use in the online course webinars. I don't know if these are the questions, but they can't really ask you many any other questions, because if it's about problem-solving, and community engagement, there's only a certain number of questions you can be asked.

How would you describe the problems that the police are facing?

How do you see your role in the position of constable in dealing with those problems?

This is where you be talking about enabling the community, forming a working group. But there's a duality here because you've got two separate things to deal with. You've got the vulnerable drug users and you've also got the individuals who are doing the drug-dealing. I'd be setting up two working groups. This is not just based on theory. I've done this. This is work I've done. Like I said, it's almost like it's written for me. In the past for a similar set of problems I formed two working groups. My role was to have a leadership position there so that I can prevent harm coming to those individuals who are suffering from drug misuse. Also, I can carry out effective enforcement against those individuals who are dealing drugs and using violence to do so.

Now, one of the questions might be something about causes:

'What are the potential causes of homelessness and drug addiction?'

This is where we start looking at not just the causes, but the causes of the causes. On top of things like Adverse Childhood Experiences, we also look at things like Adverse Adult Experiences. How do they influence your behaviour as an adult? Not just as a vulnerable person, but also as someone who's caught up in a cycle of offending?

The next question might be:

'What impact are these crimes and behaviour having on the community?'

This is where you'd be thinking about what sort of crime types of the community is suffering because of course, to be able to purchase drugs, you need money. That money doesn't grow on a tree. As a famous Prime Minister once said, 'there is no money tree.' It's got to come from somewhere and it's going to come from crime. You might also get questions about how you would, in the short term, start addressing this problem.

Then, they're going to give you developments. You're going to get four questions to start with. Like I said, you don't know what each one of these questions are until they are posed. Some of my clients talk about how they found themselves repeating themselves over and over again. Now, I think that's because you are going to give you the same sort of questions, but in respect of a development that's happened in the community.

I created a development in my case study exercise where a mother is complaining about the homelessness situation and is gathering up a groundswell of anger in the community, because her daughter found a syringe with a needle attached to it that appeared to have some blood inside the syringe. She's up in arms about that naturally and wants to have a protest and an angry meeting in the centre of town to make sure the police and other agencies do something about this problem.

You see how the scenario has developed? When you ask the question now about, 'what are the problems that the police have to face in respect of this issue?' It's the same question but about a separate issue that's just connected with the overall drug dealing and drug-taking. Again, you might get asked the question about your role in all of this. Think about what causes this sort of anger? What impact this is going to have in respect of your relationship with the community? How's it going to impact on trust? What sort of short-term actions would you take? How would you consider the safety of yourself and partner agencies in respect of any clear up of needles or any other detritus, because of drugs misuse? You're invited to that meeting. How would you manage it or is there something you could do to ensure that angry meeting doesn't happen? Is there something you can do to confront, in a very supportive way, that mother, so that you can get her involved in the working group? I get my clients to work on all these questions so I can prepare them for anything!

I also provide an example of how you could manage the angry mother using a non-contact conflict management model from the police service called CUDSAR.

This is where you confront the issue with the person. You're very specific about why you want to meet with them and support them. Then you ask them lots of questions. You can get a deeper understanding of what that problem might be and that's where we use our 5 WH skills, but also add a little bit of TED PIE. TED PIE stands for:

Tell me
Explain
Describe
Precisely
In detail
Exactly

The first three, the TED, form the first part of any question, while the PIE forms the rest. And they are interchangeable. Here are some examples:

Please can you tell me, precisely what happened?

Please can you describe, in detail the person who approach you?

Please can you explain, exactly what he was doing at the time of the incident?

Can you see how TED PIE works? There's a little tip for you. TED PIE is a 'secret' passed down from detective to detective. You won't find it if you search for it!

We go onto define and summarise the problem. Then, as opposed to telling her what the solutions are, which is the S of CUDSAR. We're going to ask the mother what she feels the best solution will be to address this issue. Then we move on to inviting her into the working group so she can help implement some of those solutions some of those ideas. We're going to assess and monitor the progress leading to a very positive result. That's the CUDSAR model.

Remember, you've got three minutes to answer each one of the questions posed and you need to fill the three minutes. You might come across some people saying, 'oh, I didn't. I only answered them using two minutes and I still passed.' But remember, we're not just after pass here. We're after an awesome mark because you might be going for one of those forces which only selects the top-scoring individuals to go through to the next stage.

In the scenario I create for my clients, the next part is where violent drug dealers are starting to ramp up the pressure in the city because they want to take better control of the drug dealing in the area. What's the problem here? How would you describe this problem? Then again, questions about the causes and the impact. What actions you would take? Unbelievably, and I know this from an ethical source, you're going to get asked a question about what actions you would take to ensure your safety and the safety of your colleagues while dealing with violent or potentially violent criminals.

You might be thinking, 'hey, I'm not even in the police yet. How am I expected to know the answer to that question?' Well, I'm with you on that one. How are you expected to know the answer to that question? I really do not know. I ran this by a retired superintendent friend of mine and he said, 'do you know that's the sort of question I'd have asked of a PC at a Sergeants Promotion Board.' I'd ask that question of someone who's an Acting Sergeant. I'd want to know what they are doing or what they're going to do to ensure the safety of themselves and their officers when dealing with violent criminality.

I wouldn't expect any of you, as potential recruits, to be able to answer that question. But if you are asked that question, you need to have an answer. Fortunately, I've provided a 15-minute long video in one of the modules in the Online Course, where I talk about things like protective equipment, radio checks, current training, all sorts of different tactics you can use for vehicle stops, drug warrants, arrest tactics, stop and search tactics.

All sorts of things that I've done over the years to ensure that both myself as a sergeant, as an inspector, and my team are safe. To make sure we all come to work with a smile on the face and all go home from work with a smile on our face. Because we've all safe. We've not been hurt. Importantly, the people we're dealing with don't get hurt as well. Because the aim is also to make sure the people you're dealing with don't get hurt. The aim is for people who are committing violent acts of criminality to be arrested safely, so that they don't get harmed as well. Because we've got a duty of care to ensure that their safety is looked after as well. Only use such force as is reasonable in the circumstances. You've got three minutes to talk about it. I provide you with 15 minutes' worth of information that you can use. That's how you nail it. You just pretend to be Brendan!

Yes, it is a ridiculous question, but the golden rule applies – 'those who hold the gold make the rules.' If the College of Policing are asking that question, there's nothing we can do to change it. All we need to do is make sure we're ahead of the game so that we can answer questions like that and score really high marks.

If this all sounds like a little bit of game playing and all sounds very formulaic in that you are just ticking boxes, you're right. You're absolutely right. There's going to be no contact with a human being during Stage 3 Briefing. You are not going to get anyone asking you questions about your values, your motivation. It's just asking questions about how you would deal with things like this if you were a police officer in this made-up location.

Now, for those of you who don't have a close social tie with the police, you're going to find this a lot harder than the people who do have a strong social tie with the police. People who are special constables or PCSOs or who have relatives and friends who are in the police and can help them prepare for situations like this. Research has shown that they have a far, far higher success rate than candidates who don't. That's where I step in.

I was only discussing this today with a positive action lead for a police force in England. We were talking about how the sort of coaching and support I provide results in the close social tie for those people who don't have those links with the police service.

I know, I'm going off tangent a little bit here, but there's a big argument here about the police just recruiting more people 'just like us.' Because people who have got close social ties to the police are more likely to be from the same ethnic group or the same religious group or the same sort of community. There is an argument that the police are actually recruiting more people 'like us' inadvertently. Is this a form of institutional discrimination?

But anyway, let's put all of that to one side because it's another subject, and one that won't really add to your ability to get through the process.

All the Online Assessment Centre - all of it is very tick-box, very formulaic. I don't think it's a very good system at all, but like I've said before, it doesn't matter what I think. All that matters is that you know what you need to do to put in the hard work and to pass it. Not just pass it, but pass it with an awesome, awesome mark. That's what we're after. We are not just after a pass. We're after a pass with a really, really high mark.

What else can you do to prepare for the Stage 3? Well, get interested in what sort of things your police force is doing to tackle anti-social behaviour and to help develop and build strong communities. What sort of community engagement strategy do they have? What sort of organisations do they work with? Have a look at case studies. Have a look at newspaper reports. Get ideas from what's going on in the force that you want to apply to. At the same time, take a look at what they're doing to tackle violent criminals. Look at what's going on all around the country with things like the Violence Reduction Units and examples of diversionary schemes such as Durham Police who have 'Checkpoint' which is quite an awesome scheme.

I provide my clients with a huge list of resources. If you ask me nicely, I might even provide you with some of those resources if you just drop me an email. If you've got any sort of questions at all, please do get in touch. It's info@bluelightconsultancy.com and I'll see what I can do to help.

But there's a lot of research that you can do without my support just to get a really good feel for how the police go about dealing with these sorts of issues. Lots of really, really good examples out there. Like I said, Durham Constabulary's Checkpoint, Thames Valley has got awesome Violence Reduction Units and there are plenty of other examples all over the country. It's down to you to research these things and use what's going on as ideas for how to tackle your Stage 3.

I hope you found this useful. Once you've got through your Online Assessment Centre, you will then be able to be invited to what most folks is called a final interview, or it could be called an in-force interview. Or it could be called a senior interview depending on what force you're applying to.

There are big variations in how these are run. The next stage I'm going to describe in the next set of chapters is not like the Online Assessment Centre. The Online Assessment Centre is something that everyone's got to do. If you're applying for a Home Office force or the Civil Nuclear Constabulary as well, you will do the Online Assessment Centre from the College of Policing. Certainly, for all forces in England and Wales. What comes next is down to the force. They don't have to follow a national model.

As an example, I've just heard about a force where before you get to the final interview, in between Online Assessment Centre and final interview, there is now a team building and a scenario-based group exercise. Now, as Covid restrictions are starting to ease, we're starting to see a return to the normal plethora of additional bits of assessment and tests of your ability that are being added to the College of Policing Assessment Centre.

Expect it to be more than just an interview. I will give you some guidance in the next set of chapters on how to deal with all these different 'interviews.' Oh yes, they might also involve role-plays. Quite a few forces have already reintroduced role-plays. The Metropolitan Police is an example of that. You might also have briefings to do. In-tray exercises to do. For many forces the next stage is so much more than just an interview.

The next set of chapters are going to prepare you for that. This is where you must stop the formulaic tick box approach for the Online Assessment Centre. This is where your real authentic and emotional self needs to come out but in a structured and detailed way. That's what we're going to look at in the next chapters.

https://bluelightonline.co.uk/book

Chapter 13 - Introduction to your Final Interview / In-Force Interview / Senior Interview

So, we've been through quite a lot of so far, and I hope you've enjoyed the chapters where we looked at the College of Policing Online Assessment Centre. I say I enjoyed it. I hope you got a lot out of it. So now we're going to look at what comes next for most forces. Remember there's over 50 different versions of getting into the police just in England and Wales alone. Add to that Police Scotland, Police Service of Northern Ireland, Ports Police, and you soon discover how there's lots of different routes you can take in the recruitment process.

For the England and Wales Home Office Forces the Online Assessment Centre is something that must happen. For other forces like Ministry of Defence Police, Civil Nuclear Constabulary, Police Scotland, Police Service of Northern Ireland, Ports Police, Isle of Man Police, States of Jersey, States of Guernsey, and others, they don't have to follow the same sort of formulaic approach. They may just have an interview with no Online Assessment Centre. You may also find that some forces put their interview before the Online Assessment Centre, but they are in the minority at this moment in time.

So, in this chapter, I'm going to introduce you to all the different types of interviews you might expect. It's hard to pin down really. I can't really give you a list of what each force does because a lot of forces change what they do on such a regular basis. Even I find it hard to keep up with all those changes and I do this full-time. This is all I do. I just focus on supporting and helping people to succeed in the police recruitment process. So, I find it difficult to keep up - I've just found out today that a force has completely changed what they do in terms of their final interview. So, in this force, before you even get to that interview, you've now got to do a team-building exercise and a scenario-based group exercise, or it might be an individual exercise. I'm not quite sure yet. I still need to find out more, but that's how fast things change. They might do that for a couple of months and then decide to do something else. So, one of the things I advocate is to prepare yourself for everything. That way, if they change what they're going to do overnight you are still going to be prepared. So, prepare for everything.

Now, whilst the Online Assessment Centre is something where you can be formulaic in your approach, it's very tick-box, the next stage isn't. Because the assessors for the Online Assessment Centre, they don't see you other than on video. They don't know who you really are. They don't even know what force you're applying for. There's nothing they will hear about your values, your motivation, what's inspired you to join, what challenges you've faced, there's none of that. They're not there to discover any of that in the Online Assessment Centre, which is why forces add on these other parts to get to the heart of why you want to join.

So, all the advice that you might hear or might read elsewhere about, 'just act naturally, just be yourself, I'm sure you'll be fine, just rely on your own character, you'll shine at the interview.' Well, I'm not sure about that advice. We need to prepare. We do need to really prepare for the final interview as this is this is the last hurdle for many of you apart from things like medical and vetting and fitness.

So, you've got to get it right. And this is where it's not going to be College of Policing assessors who are remote from the force, who are going to be choosing whether you are the right person for their force. It's going to be real police officers and police officers who are out on the streets at this moment on the front line of policing. Forces like to use serving police officers who are out on the front line, sergeants, inspectors, chief inspectors, and I even heard last week that a chief constable had stepped in to do some interviews (that's very rare!). What happens most of the time is you're going to be interviewed by someone who's of the rank of Inspector, Chief Inspector or it could be a Sergeant. I did hear today how one of my clients was interviewed by one chief inspector, two constables and an officer from the HR team. Invariably there will be someone there from HR as well.

So, it can appear quite daunting, but when you prepare and you practice and you rehearse, you'll come across on the day as being confident. You'll be able to talk in a conversational way and that's what they're going to be looking for. Someone who can come across in an authentic way, but still being able to talk about the emotional impact of things. Someone who can talk about their self in a way that is structured and full of detail.

Typically most final interviews, when it's just questions being asked, can last anything from 45 minutes to an hour. In that time, they might ask you seven or eight questions. So, just do the math. Do the math. Each answer that you give needs to be a good four minutes or so. At the very least, if you can talk for four or five minutes about the scenario that you're explaining, then you're in a good position.

Whenever people come to me and they've already gone through the process but failed their final interview, I'll ask them questions about how long their interview was meant to be, '45 minutes to an hour,' they'll say. I'll then say, 'I bet your interview was over in 20 to 25 minutes.' They'll look at me in amazement and say, 'how did you know that?' Of course, I knew, they'd not given enough detail and have not given enough about themselves for the assessors to decide as to whether they are the sort of individual who can work for them. Think about it this way, on your final interview you are getting the opportunity to have a discussion, to have a conversation, with the sort of people that you might be working with one day. Indeed, you might be, you might be on their shift in 12 months' time.

So, the other questions they're going to be asking themselves, and these won't be on the marking guide are:

'Can I see this person fitting into my team? Because if I say yes to them today, they might well be on my team in 12 months' time.'

'Can I see them at three o'clock in the morning after they've already been working for 10 to 12 hours, pulling another 'rabbit out the hat' and going to another difficult challenging and complex incident?

'They might be working 16 or 17 hours overnight – are they going to complain?'

'Are they going to give 120% without being asked to do so?'

'Are they are going to volunteer for incidents?'

'Are they are going to be positive, to show determination and resilience?'

'They're going to make great decisions and sometimes make mistakes. But will they make those mistakes with humility, and will they approach me so we can talk about it, so it doesn't fester and become a massive mistake?'

'Is this the sort of person I can see on my team?'

That's the final question they're asking themselves either on a conscious level or on an unconscious level. I know that because I've been that interviewer. I've seen people walk through the door, and I've written them off within seconds of them walking through the door. You might be thinking, 'well, that's a bit unfair, isn't it?' But when you've got someone coming in who hasn't shaved that day, half their shirt is hanging out of their trousers, hasn't put any polish on their shoes, the trousers look like they've been dragged through a hedge backwards, they wipe their nose on their hand and then offer their hand to me to be shaken, I don't think so! I remember thinking of him as the 'snot monster' because of what he offered me on his hand. Straight away I thought, 'this person doesn't care. This person hasn't got the courtesy to turn up looking smart. So, I don't care how good the interview is, they're not getting into my Constabulary, they're not joining Greater Manchester Police. Unfortunately for my own bias their interview was a complete train wreck, and they did fail.

So, first impressions do count. Which is why one of the questions that's often asked at the very beginning is this one. By the way, they might also say, 'it's just a warm-up question - this one isn't being formally assessed.' Don't be taken in by that one. That's a trap. I'll talk about more traps you might fall into in the next chapters, but that's one of the big traps. So, this is the question that isn't being marked formally, 'so why do you want to be a police officer?"

They've already told you this question is not being marked. Oh yes, it is. It might not be formally marked but you're making an impression and they are going to make subjective decisions about you. Why am I saying subjective? Well, because they're human. They've got their own biases. They can't help it because they're human. All the decisions that the assessors make at this point as interviewers are going to be subjective decisions, which is why someone from HR is there to try and make sure that those subjective decisions about your performance in your interview are as objective as possible. You may be thinking, 'well, that's not fair,' but the alternative is the Online Assessment Centre on its own, which is very, very objective. But doesn't do anything to evaluate and assess your motivation and values. Whereas the final interview does.

So, what else might the final interview have in store for you. We're going to explore all these things in the next chapters. So, one of the first questions you might be asked is, 'why do you want to be a police officer and why this force?' We might not get asked that question. They might just go straight into competency type questions but it's always good to know your why. And in the next chapter, we're going to start off by looking at your why.

You could get asked questions about values that are important to you, values that are important to police officers. You could get asked questions about the impact of being a police officer on your personal life. They could ask you questions about your knowledge of the force and your understanding of policing challenges that exist at national level, force level and locally. They'll expect you to know more about the force then they do.

They could also and probably will ask you competency-based questions. These are the ones that start off with, 'can you tell me about a time when....'

They could also ask you forward-facing questions. These are questions where they will say things like, 'so if you were faced with a police officer who said something inappropriate, how would you deal with them?' Or, 'how will you ensure that you take into consideration diversity, equality, and inclusion issues once you're a police officer?' There's one force that recently had that as a 10-minute presentation.

You could be given scenario-based questions where they give you a detailed scenario and then say, 'How would you deal with this?' You could be given a group exercise where you're all given individual pieces of information and the only way you can solve the problem is if you all come together and share that information, so you can come up with decisions about how you're going to deal with the issue that you faced with.

You could be faced with role plays. The role plays might put you in a position of a police officer or they might put you in the position of a security officer or they could put you in the position of a council neighbourhood warden. I've seen all those types of role plays run recently. I've just heard one force is now introduced a team-building exercise. I have no idea what that's going to involve but it'd be interesting to find out. A lot of forces will ask you to do a presentation and they'll give you the topic beforehand or a choice of topics beforehand. The trap you might fall into there is the PowerPoint trap. Don't use PowerPoint, that's my top tip. Anyway, more about that later. Especially for the Detective Direct Entry route, where you could get an in-tray exercise, a briefing exercise, or both!

So, there's a lot there to think about, and in the next set chapters, I'm going to give you an introduction to how to deal with all those types of final interview questions. Like I said before, it could be called a senior interview, or it could be called the in-force interview, or it could be called an additional assessment. It could be called all sorts of different things.

In any case, I'm really looking forward to sharing my knowledge and understanding, which has been developed over a quarter of a century of advising, supporting and guiding people just like you to deal with all these sorts of scenarios. Because one thing is certain, none of them are new. All of what I've just talked about are things that have been used for years as far as I can remember.

In my 1994 sergeant's board, I was given an in-tray exercise. In my sergeant's board there was a group exercise. In my sergeant's board there were scenario-based questions and competency type of questions, as well as motivation and values type questions.

So, none of these are new ideas, which is helpful as there are structures we can utilise and methods we can learn to best prepare ourselves for any of those likelihoods. So, I'm looking forward to that.

If you've got any questions, as always, just drop me a line at info@bluelightconsultancy.com and I'll do my best to answer those questions for you. In the next chapter we're going to look at motivation and values.

https://bluelightonline.co.uk/book

Chapter 14 - Your motivation and inspiration to join the Police Service – exploring your 'Why?'

Following on from the introductory Chapter to the final interview stage, sometimes called senior interview or in-force interview, we're going to start looking at all the different types of questions you could get asked.

Starting with, what is probably the hardest question, 'why do you want to be a police officer?

So many of you struggle with this and when I do my one-to-one coaching or the webinars, the interactive webinars for those people who have purchased the interview course, invariably when asked this question, even though there's a long module on this in the interview course, people tend to refer to cliches.

Things like:

'I've always wanted to be a police officer.'

No, you haven't actually.

'No two days are the same.'

Well, if everyone says that, does that make you different in any way?

'I just want to put something back into the community.'

Right, great. What have you done so far?

'I just want to help people.'

Super, what you've done so far?

'I want to serve my community.'

Great, what have you done so far?

So, these are some of the cliches I hear often. There's a tendency for people to come out with these and I don't know why. Perhaps, there's some book out there that advises you to say those things? And then they go into even more cliches such as, 'I share the same values as the police service.' Oh dear!

So, we want to avoid cliches like that because if everyone's saying those things, then it doesn't really tell them anything about you. This opening question is one that has a quite a deep purpose, even if they say to you that this question is not being marked, trust me, it is at an unconscious level.

So it may not be being marked formally on their marking guide, but it has been marked in their heads. They're deciding as to what sort of person you are based on the answer to this question. If you just roll off some cliches, it tells them nothing about you. Nothing about your values, nothing about your motivation, nothing about what or who has inspired you.

It doesn't enable you to come across as the individual that you need to come across, one that is authentic, one that's emotional, one that really has this strong desire to be a police officer.

So, the way we get around avoiding those cliches is to tell a story. Tell a story, one that is unique to you. A story that is unique and about you.

And for that purpose, what I recommend is to use a timeline.

So, if you think back to that moment in time when you were inspired, someone or something inspired you to be a police officer. You didn't just wake up one morning and think, 'I know what I'll do. I'll be a police officer.' It doesn't work like that. If I cast my mind back to what inspired me? The first thing was my grandfather who taught me much and told me to get a grip on my life. I can remember him saying to me how I need to do something useful as, 'at the moment, you're not doing anything.' He then talked about my Uncle George who had passed away at that point, bless his soul, but who was a Chief Inspector in Staffordshire Constabulary. He talked about how he thought that might be an interesting career for me and he was right. It was an interesting career.

The other inspiration was when I was 18 and got thrown in a hedge by an inspector!

I was walking home from a party, rather drunk, in the early hours and a police car came past. I eyeballed the police car and of course, police officers back in the early 80s didn't like being eyeballed and this was an inspector. He slammed the brakes on, jumped out of the car and grabbed hold of me. He then went on to ask me what I was doing. I told him it had nothing to do with him, it was none of his business, causing him to promptly throw me into a hedge! He then dragged me out again and told me I look like a burglar. I challenged him back and said, 'well, better arrest me then!' He threw me back in the hedge again and told me how he didn't want to see me again that evening.

Now, feeling rather indignant, I marched off to the local police station, Cheadle Hulme Police Station in Stockport. I wanted to complain about this inspector's behaviour and so I went to the front desk, and yes, back then they had police officers on the front desk at night-time in small stations, like Cheadle Hulme. And there was a police officer there who was not much older than me. I said, 'I want to complain about your inspector,' followed by why. I can still remember her saying, 'not him again, he's like that with us, but stops short of throwing us in hedges.'

I thought that was a pretty cool answer. So, I started to get into conversation with her, asking questions about what it was really like to be a police officer, what sort of things she gets up to and what does she think of the job?

And that's when I started thinking, do you know, this might be for me. I also remember asking her for leaflets or guidance on joining. She said, 'well, not to join the regulars but I've got piles of leaflets here for the special constabulary, but that's not the same.' But still, it left me thinking how this sounded like an interesting career. Anyway, those were the two moments.

So, I've not always wanted to be a police officer. Actually, I wanted to be a doctor of all things early on in my life. Well, I think my parents wanted me to be a doctor, but that's where the story starts. So, who or what inspired you? And I know some of you are going to be thinking, 'I can't think. I can't think.' I get this all the time, especially on my 1-2-1 coaching sessions.

People will say, I can't think of that moment, and I'll ask them certain questions and they will answer those certain questions in their mind and a couple minutes later they'll go, 'yes, it was my friend's neighbour,' or their father was a police officer, or they got chatting to a police officer once and heard stories of…

It will always be something like that, or it could be how they watched something happen in real life involving the police, watched it unfold, and was amazed at how the police officers were, X type of character or value. There's always a moment in time that sets that seed. However, it doesn't mean to say that at that moment, you decided, 'I've got to be a police officer.'

But that's the moment in time that started your journey. So, it's almost like you're telling a story that starts with, 'once upon a time,' where my friend introduced me to his father who was a police officer, and that's when it all starts.

Of course, you don't say, 'once upon a time,' but you can start your answer with, 'it all started with....' or actually, one or two of my clients have made the interviewer smile when they've said things like, 'I've not always wanted to be a police officer, you know.' Almost as if to say, I know what you're expecting from most candidates is just a lot of cliches, but you're not going to get that from me!

What I do then is to follow up the initial inspiration with all the different steps in their timeline, the steps taken to investigate, to research, to find out more and the things that they've done to start preparing themselves for a career in the police.

So, you want to put something back into the community. Great, what sort of things have you done? Have you done some volunteering? Then mention it and what it taught you and how that skill is transferable to the police.

Push yourself to take on a position of responsibility in the workplace, or to find opportunities to help support people in the workplace or elsewhere. Just saying, 'I just want to help people' in an interview answer isn't enough, demonstrate what you have done to help people and tell the interviewers what you discovered about yourself that is relevant to the role of a constable.

What have you done to demonstrate that you are a strong character? Because strong characters can stand up for themselves. Actually, what the police are really looking for is the stronger character because, while the strong character can stand up for themselves, it's the stronger character that stands up for those who can't stand up for themselves.

What have you done to support people who may be getting bullied? What have you done to reach out to people who no one else is talking to for some reason, the outsider? What are you doing to offer the hand of friendship to all, no matter what their background is or their social status? Those are not my words, that's Sir Robert Peel, the founder of the police service back in 1829.

We talked about the role of a police officer is to offer friendship to all. So, what are you doing? What have you done? And then when you've done those things, how did it make you feel? Did it give you this realisation that actually, that felt good, that felt really, really good? It made you realise that you want to fill your life with more of these types of experiences?

In your answer you are describing a journey of self-actualisation, when you realise what your purpose is, when you realise the difference between success and fulfilment.

Often in a career or in your studies, you can be really successful, but your role might not be giving you the fulfilment that you need in your life. I find this a lot with my clients who, when we have in-depth 1-2-1's they talk about their current career and how they might be successful in it, or successful in their studies, but it's not providing the fulfilment that something else in their life does, which is what further inspired them to want to join the police service.

Now, in addition to thinking these things through, I'd also like you to try and find serving police officers to talk to. There are a few police forces out there who give you an extra mark if you do this. It's on their marking guide for questions about your motivation, or what you have done to find out more about the role. Has the candidate spoken to serving officers?

So as part of your 'why' answer, I'd highly recommend you get to speak to serving officers. You might be thinking, 'I don't know any.' Well, reach out to all your friends and relatives, because I'm quite sure one of them will know someone who's a serving or retired officer. If that doesn't work, just go to your local police station, and just ask, 'is there someone I can speak to?' Take doughnuts, take cakes, they love that.

Now, you might be thinking, well, what if they say, no? What if they say, they haven't got the time? Well, they might do. They might say that. One of my clients, who was transferring from the Ministry of Defence Police, he did this. He wanted to join the Merseyside Police. He's in Merseyside Police now.

He went to one police station in the morning and got a, 'we've not got time for that type of thing,' reply, and so he went back in the afternoon when he knew a different shift would be on duty. They also said, 'no, that's not the sort of thing we do. You need to call recruitment for that.' And so, he thought, 'right then. Well, I'm not going to let that get in the way.'

So, he went to a different police station a few miles away and knocked on their door and asked the question, 'is there anyone that I could talk to? I'm hoping to transfer from the Ministry of Defence Police into your force.' You could just say the same thing that you're hoping to join the police and you've got your interview coming up at some point in the future.

He mentioned how it'd be good to be able to speak to a police officer to find out what it's really like to be a police officer in Merseyside. For a lot of you, you might want to ask for someone who is younger in service because they were like you just a year before. For my client who went knocking on a door on that station, bingo, it worked out perfectly for him.

He got welcomed in and shown around. He got to meet the sergeant and a group of constables. He got to meet the inspector who talked to him for 30 minutes about the role of a PC. He came up with loads of good things that you could weave into his answers in terms of why'd you want to believe a police officer and why Merseyside. Interesting approach.

He also got a phone call from HR to say, 'have you've been knocking on the doors of police stations asking questions about being a police officer?' and he replied, 'yes.' 'Who said you could do that?' they asked him in return. His reply was awesome, 'well, who said I couldn't?' I thought that was a great answer – typical police!

Anyways, he's in the police now, so do it. Some forces, like I said, give you an extra mark for doing that kind of research.

There you go, folks. There's a lot to do there, isn't there? There is a lot to do. You thought it would be really simple, that all you would need to say about why you want to be a police officer is how, 'I've always wanted to.... No two days are the same, my values align with....' Just no, you come up with all those cliches, you're just going to sound like everyone else, and you'll probably fail.

Tell your unique story because every one of you is unique. All of you have got a unique inspiration, unique motivation for wanting to be a police officer. Now, think deeply about this. Remember, it's competitive and the person who's interviewing you is always thinking, 'can I see this person on my team?' 'Can I see them at three o'clock in the morning pulling another 'rabbit out of the hat,' giving 120% without being asked to do so, being one of our heroes because that's what police officers are.

You know, I think the police are awesome. I love them. I love them all for what they do to protect us.

So, there you go. Your big why, start working on that and if you get this answer right, it sets you up for the rest of the interview. So, in terms of the rest of the interview, I'll catch you at the next chapter.

https://bluelightonline.co.uk/book

Chapter 15 - How to structure your Competency and Values Interview Answers

This chapter is going to focus on competency-type questions for your final interview, which is going to be the backbone of most interviews. I've not actually heard of one interview for any force that takes place without any form of competency-related questions.

Now, these are sort of questions that start off with, 'can you tell me about a time when....?' So, we've covered some of that for the Online Assessment Centre, but now we're going to cover the sort of depth and difference you're going to need to prepare for the final interview. And what I recommend is that you prepare for every type of question.

So for every one of the values, for every one of the competencies, you should come up with answers to the sample questions I provide on the Bluelight Interview Question Bank (part of my online course). I'm going to give you some examples of these in this chapter. If you want to access the full range of questions of course, that's all available on Bluelight's Interview Course, together with explainer videos for every one of the values and competencies. So much information there, you can't go wrong. Check out the Offer Wall at the end of this chapter for more (the Platinum package, which also gives you access to unlimited practice webinars as well as recordings of previous ones).

How should you approach these types of questions? Well, first, you'll be looking at an answer that's about 4 or 5 minutes long. We just need to do the math about how long your final interview is going to be - typically, it's going to be anything from forty-five minutes to an hour. One or two forces try to squeeze it all in the space of thirty minutes, but typically it's forty-five minutes to an hour and it should become very conversational.

But that also means that your answers need to be sufficiently long and sufficiently detailed to be able to fill that forty-five minute to an hour period. So, what I recommend is that you should be looking for answers that are in the range of 4 to 5 minutes long, without adding things that are just unnecessary. Because just to fill 4 or 5 minutes, it needs to be all the detail that will ensure that your answer meets the marking guide.

This interview is also where you've really got to be your authentic and emotional self in a very structured and detailed way. Because remember, the people who are interviewing you at this point, are serving police officers. They're out on the frontline now, they're detective inspectors, neighbourhood inspectors, response inspectors and firearms inspectors. They may also work as detectives in areas that support vulnerable people or in specialist roles like Special Branch.

As I said before, typically they're going to be inspectors, but they could be sergeants, they could be a chief inspector, or (rarely) a superintendent. But typically, they're going to be an Inspector, and they're out in the front line now. And they don't get to the rank of Inspector by collecting tokens from Coco Pops packets, they get to the rank of Inspector because they're good-people people. They understand people, they can sense when someone's telling them something that's not quite right, they can sense when someone's over-egging the pudding, they can sense when someone's giving them just a sample answer from some book they have read. Yes, there are books out there that provide (really poor!) sample interview answers.

I remember in a 1-2-1 with one of my clients, how five minutes into the session he said to me how he was thinking about just inventing some answers. As soon as he said this, that was the end of our relationship. Because I knew that he would, one, get found out and two, he just told me he intends to lie. And I'm not going to work with people like that.

So, whatever you do, don't make things up. It's got to be about your past. If it's not, these inspectors, sergeants and chief inspectors will work it out straight away. They'll be straight on to you, they'll discover your deceit, and then they will fail you. So please don't go down that road. Tempting it might be to over-egg the pudding, to embellish your account. Don't. Speak from your heart, speak from what happened and you're not going to go wrong.

Other poor advice I've seen elsewhere, especially in the Bluelight Facebook group, makes me cringe every time I see it. When someone says, 'has anyone got any advice for the final interview?' I'll see replies like, 'just know your competencies or learn your competencies.' That's not really going to help you. Learning what they are, parrot-fashion, is not going to help you. Knowing how to utilise the Competency and Values Framework to construct possible questions that you're going to get asked is what will help you. And from there work out what supplementary points you need to include in your answer. By doing this you can meet the behavioural statements within those values and within those competencies.

Don't worry if you don't understand what I've just said too much, because you don't need to do all that work. I've done it for you, and I'm going to give you some examples of the sort of questions you're going to get asked in the next chapter. I'm also going to provide guidance for each one of the questions in terms of what you need to include in your answer. How do I do this? I've examined the values and the competencies and the behavioural statements within the values and the competencies. From this I've been able to formulate possible interview questions that they're going to ask you as well as the supplementary points you should include in your answer.

I've also taken the behaviours, which sometimes are written in 'competency speak,' and I've turned them into something called, 'Plain English' for you, so that you can actually understand exactly what it is that they're looking for in the answer. That'll make more sense when I tell you what sort of questions you're going to get asked and what you need to cover.

Other things to avoid. There's guidance out there, I know this because I've seen it, that tells you to use words and phrases from the Competency and Values Framework in your answers.

That is a big 'No!'

If you start using buzzwords from the Competency and Values Framework, you will annoy the interviewers. Let me give you an example. So, if you said something in an answer like, 'I worked in a collaborative way with my fellow team members, ensuring that I was meeting organisational aims and objectives at the same time.'

Sounds great, isn't it?

However, it's absolutely meaningless. So as an interviewer, I'd be on all over that comment at the end of your answer, where I would ask you, 'so, you said you worked collaboratively with the rest of your team. How did you do that? How exactly did you do that?' So, if you try and use any big buzzwords with me, I'm going to make a note of them and they're going to haunt you at the end of your answer. I'm going to ask you to explain how exactly how you did those buzzwords things.

You're just going to annoy the interviewer if you start using buzzwords, especially if they're buzzwords from the Competency and Values Framework. You might be thinking, 'Well, how will they understand that I've worked collaboratively with others? The answer is to describe how you worked with other people and let them make the judgment that what you did was collaborative. So, avoid buzzwords, please avoid, avoid, avoid the buzzwords.

You will also need a structure, and I provide a detailed template for that structure in the online course. A very detailed one to enable you to be able to talk for 5 minutes. I'm also going to introduce you to the basics of that structure now.

If you search for, 'How to answer interview questions,' your search engine is going to bring up something called, STAR.' I don't know why STAR is so popular, maybe it's because it is also a word? It stands for Situation, Task, Action, and Result.

The problem is, I don't know many people who can explain the difference between the Task and Actions. What most people say are things like, 'well, the task is what I set out to do and the action is what I did.'

Confusing, isn't it?

Or, 'I was tasked to do something and then the actions were what I did to complete the task I was set.' Well, if I'm an interviewer, I don't really want to hear about tasks you're set. I want to hear about times when you've given 120% without being asked to do so, where you have shown the initiative.

So don't say that you were tasked to do something because your answer will just be about you following directions, you just did what you were asked to do. Nothing remarkable about that at all. I want you to give me examples of times in your professional or personal life that have been particularly challenging, that have been particularly difficult. I want to hear about when you've pushed yourself.

So that's where I think the STAR model gets people a little bit confused. Also, no one ever really talks like that, do they? No one says things like, 'so I tasked myself up with....' Who talks like that? Anyone? I don't. So, let's not start talking in a way that we don't normally because that'll throw you as well. You're not going to come across as your authentic self.

And sometimes, at the end of that STAR, people will add an 'E' for 'Evaluate.' That makes it the 'STARE model.' I've got a problem with that as well. No one says things like, 'I evaluated my performance, I evaluated the way I completed that task.' No one talks like that. So don't start talking like that in your interview.

What tends to happen in the interview, by the way, is there might be a bit of an introduction, you know, 'how did you get here?' Or, 'where do you come from today?' What the interviewer is doing there is chitchat with you so that you get comfortable talking to them. And then they might ask questions like those we covered before about, 'why do you want to join the police? Why do you want to join this force?' These questions are there to get you talking.

As you give your answers they might start thinking, 'this is going really well. This is very conversational. This person seems to be very bright, dynamic, and enthusiastic.'

And then they ask the first big question of the interview, 'So can you tell me about a time when you've worked with other people to solve a problem?' And you turn into 'robot CVF' mode and you start using phrases like, 'So I tasked myself up with... I evaluated my performance,' and the interviewer is sat there thinking, 'what's happened to that person we met before? Suddenly they've become weird, they're talking oddly.'

I know that because I've been that interviewer. So, let's avoid all of these problems by using a completely different model. This is one I've developed over decades. Actually, I've played around with all sorts of different models to answer police interview questions and have used them in my own development over the years, to get promoted, to get into specialist departments, and in my coaching of others.

The model I have settled on is called SAARLKU. I know it sounds a bit of a mouthful and it doesn't spell a word, but it works. It has worked for 1000's of people just like you.

The SAARLKU model goes like this. There's more to it by the way, each one of the headings has a whole load of little subheadings, but you'll need my template for that.

So, the first part is Situation.

This is how you would start this stage of your answer:

'In my role as a XXXXX, at XXXXX, which is an organisation which does XXXXX, a specific situation occurred where....'

That's how you start off every one of your answers. You might also want to explain what the organisation you belong to does, and what that role that you're in does, because they can't read your minds, and they don't know about life in the army or life as an accountant or life in retail. They're police officers, they know what life as a police officer is like, they don't know about the rest.

So first, you are describing the situation - you might also want to start thinking about the problem that you are describing here. You're setting the scene. And so, if that problem wasn't addressed, what would be the impact on you, your organisation, your team, other individuals involved?

Aim

And now is opposed to task, we're going to think about our 'Aim' because in solving the problem or issue, you are aiming to achieve something.

When you started thinking about how you needed to address this problem or issue, start thinking of it in terms of, 'what was I aiming to achieve? Now we're thinking about what we were aiming to achieve, we can start thinking about, 'what options did I have to enable me to achieve that aim?' Does that make sense? I think it makes sense to a lot of people because I've had feedback from thousands to say that this worked for them.

Recently, I had feedback from a Chief Inspector, actually, they're not a Chief Inspector anymore, they're a Superintendent. They heard me talking about SAARLKU on one of my podcasts and used it at their promotion board. They gave me some great feedback, 'I've just got promoted to Superintendent. First time I use this model, it's awesome. Thank you.' You're welcome, Superintendent! So, we're going to talk about our aim and then two or three options we've considered to achieve that aim.

The option that you're always going to settle on is you decided to tackle this yourself, because if you settled on the option which is, 'I decided to refer it to my manager,' well, that's it, it's the end of the answer, isn't it? But it's always an option though. So, talk about your options. One of the other options might have been getting someone else to help you or watching someone else deal with whatever it is so that you could learn from them.

But again, both of those options don't enable you to go any further with your answer. So, the option is always going to be that you decided to deal with it yourself. Probably, because of a sense of urgency and how the right time to deal with it was now and how dealing with the problem could not to be put it off to the next day because of certain issues.

So now we've described the situation in detail, the impact on others, what we're aiming to achieve, the options that we considered, and the option that we settled on as well as our rationale for choosing that option.

Actions

Now, we can start talking about the actions we took. So that's the second 'A' of the SAARLKU model. Now, here is where most people fall down. They fall down because they talk more about what they did, but not about how they actually did those things.

Here's an example:

'I approached the person calmly and professionally. I sat next to them and listened to them empathetically.'

All those phrases sound great, but they're completely meaningless unless you explain how you did those things. And trust me, in my webinars, for group webinars, and for individual one-to-one coaching, I probably spend about fifty percent of the time focusing on developing people's ability, my client's ability to describe the 'how.'

And it's not their fault, and it's not your fault neither, because no one has ever taught you this at college or university or school. Not being aware of good interview technique - it's not your fault. So, people will go into the interview, making all those bold claims as to what they did but not how they did it. It's the how' that's important.

On my online course and on my webinar, I do with an exercise with people called, 'The 7 levels of how.' It starts off with someone saying something like,

Client: 'So I spoke to the rest of my teammates and found out what the issues were.'

Me: 'Spoke to your teammates. Great, how did you do that?'
Client: 'Well, I had a meeting.'

Me: 'You had a meeting. How did you do that?'

And it goes deeper and deeper, and deeper, and deeper – for 7 levels, until we get to the fine granular detail of how they did 'spoke to.'

It's awesome. When we do the '7 levels of how' it's so revealing. Normally, by about the sixth or fifth level, people are starting to get it and they start to think, 'all right. Now, I get it. I need to describe specifically the types of questions I asked, and why, and how I listened to that individual.'

So, make sure you also describe in detail not just what you did, but how you did it.

Result

So now we move into the Result. Now, there's a lot of guidance out there that says how you should use examples of where what you did was successful. However, you're going to join the police. Can I share with you that just about every plan you have in the police, every plan I've had in the police to achieve something hasn't worked out perfectly? Plans in the police rarely work out as you thought they might.

What you intend to achieve, invariably, isn't what you actually achieve. Why? Because policing is a fast-moving dynamic world that involves people. Once you introduce people into the formula, everything starts getting very confusing. And so, you have to deal with that confusion. People don't do what you ask them to do, or if you ask someone to do something, they do something completely different. People don't always report back to you, people don't turn up when they said they're going to turn up.

The world of policing is about dealing with problems in a very dynamic way. So, in your answers I don't want to hear about examples of when something is gone awesomely for you, where everything you touch 'turns to gold' and everything in your garden is rosy. Why? Because I'm going to think two things, one, the situation wasn't very challenging, or two, you're lying and what you are telling me, didn't really happen like that.

Let's focus on why the result shouldn't be perfect and what you were hoping to achieve. Because if it went so well, the first time you dealt with this situation, then clearly, it wasn't very challenging for you, it wasn't very difficult for you to deal with.

I want to hear about difficult, challenging situations, where the situation generated some emotion, some frustration maybe. How did you manage those frustrations? Tell the interviewers. This is how we fill a 4- or 5-minute answer.

For the result phase, I'd like you to think about the 80/20 rule. I often think about how 80% of what you did went to plan and 20% didn't. Now you can describe how that 20% impacted the overall result. And you can also then take that 20% of what didn't go right and use it in the next stage.

I'm using that 80/20 principle, it could be 90/10, or it could be 70/30. Just as long as in your answer there is genuinely something that didn't go to plan. And there will be, because if you're describing to the interviewer something that was a challenging situation for you, that you had not dealt with before, that you felt nervous about initially, or felt frustrated about or certain other emotions, then I'm not going to expect it to turn out 100% brilliant. I'm going to expect there to be a result where it wasn't what you planned, or it wasn't perfect.

Learning

And so, from there, we can talk about your learning. Now, learning isn't saying things like, 'I learned that it's good to talk. I learned that it's good to plan ahead. I learned that is good to use open questions.' No, those are just statements of fact. Real learning is when you reflect and think about what didn't go to plan. What was the cause of it not going to plan? What can I do differently next time if the same situation occurred, or if I could go back in time and deal with the same thing again, what is it I would do differently to ensure that the things that didn't go to plan went to plan?

So give the interviewers some detailed and meaningful learning.

Knowledge and Understanding

Now we move into the KU - this is the icing on the cake. If you stop at the learning, you'll already have delivered an awesome answer. I can promise you that. An awesome one, especially, if you follow my more detailed interview course template. The KU stands for 'knowledge and understanding.' So, if your answer is about working collaboratively with others, you could say: 'And this is an important skill set for police officers because I realise that once I'm in the police, most of what I do will involve working with other people especially people from the partner agencies.

So my understanding of how I will go about doing that is as follows. Whenever I get the opportunity to speak to someone from a partner agency, I'll ask them about the sort of issues they are faced with daily and maybe, how I can help them to meet those issues?'

By adding the knowledge and understanding steps you are explaining why the value or competency is so important and as well as demonstrating how you would implement it once in service. There's a whole module in the interview online course where I discuss how knowledge and understanding applies to each one of the values and competencies. So, plenty there for you, to practice.

One of the things I need you to do to get good at answering interview questions, to develop your proficiency, is to practice, practice, practice, and reflect on your performance. Record yourself, play yourself back, and start thinking about how that came across. Practice with anyone you can find that will practice with you.

Within the Bluelight Facebook Client Groups, there are always people putting a shout-out to say, 'is there anyone available who'd like to practice interview questions with me?' They go on to do things like set up their own Zoom sessions, which I think is awesome. I mean, what an awesome community this is! If you're not part of that community yet, get part of it. This is for you if you're thinking, 'I've got no one to practice with.' Or whenever you do practice with someone, they just laugh at you or they don't understand.

In the Bluelight Community, you've got people who were on the same courses as you. They've got the same dilemmas as you, they're going through the same challenges, and they've got the same prize at the end of it, they want that warrant card in their pocket. I cannot over emphasise the value in practicing with other people. Writing answers down is just the start of the journey, practicing them with real people is where the real practice comes in, the real preparation. And that's why the webinars I run are so effective because you get to practice with me. I know what works and I know what doesn't work.

So there you go, folks, an introduction to competency-type questions. In the next chapter, I'm going to give you some examples of what those questions are, and what the supplementary points might be for those questions. So, I hope you've got a lot out of this one. You may need to read it back a few times and make more notes and that's okay, it's not all going to sink in straight away.

https://bluelightonline.co.uk/book

Chapter 16 - How to answer 'Forward Facing' questions

In this chapter, I'm going to take a look at what are often called forward-facing questions. In the last chapter, we looked at questions which are very much based on the CVF, the ones that start with, 'can you tell me about a time when......?'

Forward-facing questions are the opposite of that because they will ask about how you will do something in the future. So, with forward-facing questions, we're still going to use the same answer structure. We're just going to adapt it a little bit. We're also going to use a model which I really like from Simon Sinek, who's an organisational development thought leader. He developed came up something called the 'Sinek Circles' (check it out on YouTube) where he talked about the marketing of an idea or concept. His model involves you explaining the 'Why' first, then the 'How,' then the 'What.' Seriously, it's well worth watching his now famous video on this. So, we're going to adapt this to start thinking about Why this behaviour or skill is so important, How we would implement it and What it will result in. This is going to enable you to deliver a powerful answer.

Now, before any of you start panicking a little bit about forward-facing questions, they're not asked by every force, and they don't often crop up, but I always think it's good to be prepared for them just in case one does.

So, the sort of questions that you might get:

How will you engage with the community in the future?

How will you work collaboratively in the future with partner organisations?

How will you support diversity, equality, and inclusion issues?

How will you deal with inappropriate behaviour demonstrated by colleagues?

How will you go about making decisions?

How will you go about solving problems within community settings?

Some of those questions might be freaking you out a little bit, with you thinking how you don't know the answers to them.
Well, you won't be expected to know the answers to them now, but as with what I explained in the last chapter, the more we prepare, the more we rehearse, the more we develop and practice, the easier these sorts of questions become to answer. I'm not expecting supercop answers, the sort of answers that an inspector or sergeant will be able to deliver, they recognise that you are a potential recruit.

So, they're just looking for some promise. They're just looking to see whether you've done your research. So, let's break down those questions. First, engaging with the community. You'd start off with just by describing why it's important to do community engagement - when you do your research, you should be finding out why the police service do community engagement.

What is the purpose behind it? The basic purpose behind community engagement is to solve problems, to enable community members to solve problems wherever they can, and to support them in doing so. And where they can't deal with those problems themselves, to ensure you work collaboratively. So, how do the police in your chosen force work collaboratively with partner organisations, to ensure that the problems within communities are resolved?

So these are the sort of things that I'd expect you to know about because you've researched them. In my online course, I point you in the right direction as to where to research these sorts of issues. It is a big list!

Similarly, with diversity, equality, and inclusion. You need to be more than just aware of these issues, you need to be able to discuss them. Derbyshire Constabulary even go as far as asking you to do a presentation on the importance of diversity, equality, and inclusion.

So now is the time to start researching these issues within the policing sector and to get interested in what's going on currently. Join Twitter and follow the National Black Police Association as well as any other staff associations, particularly for the force that you want to apply to, that support people from minority groups. This is going to enable you to have a great understanding of diversity, equality, and inclusion issues and why they are so important to the police service.

Very basically, diversity, equality and inclusion are important because the police service needs to reflect the communities they should be a part of. If the police service doesn't look and feel like the communities they are serving, then we've got a situation where the police seem like they're apart from the community as opposed to a part of the community.

When you have people from the communities within the area that the police serve, then there's a greater understanding of all those sorts of issues that get brought up by either cultural or religious, or to do with gender issues, or sexual preference. When people can talk about those issues within the service because they are represented within the service, and people from the communities can see that they're represented within the service, then we are getting closer to Sir Robert Peel's vision for what the police should be.

Remember, the police are the public and the public are the police, this is one of the Peelian Principles. There's another line that comes after that and there's a little prize if anyone can tell me what that is without looking it up!

So anyway, I digress a little bit. In terms of dealing with inappropriate behaviour, you should know the answer to that as well because within The Code of Ethics, it tells you what your responsibility is if you were to witness inappropriate behaviour from a fellow police officer or police staff. So again, this is something that you should be aware of because you can research these sorts of issues.

How will you make decisions in the future? You'll be looking to the National Decision Model. This is how the police service and individuals within the police service, go about decision-making. You would be expected to be able to describe how the National Decision Model might work in a specific context.

So, I would be a big fan of following what goes on within your force and looking for some difficult real-life scenarios that you can apply the NDM to.

Lastly, how would you go about solving problems? Here, you'd be expected to know all about the SARA problem-solving methodology. If you've been in my online assessment centre course, you'll have gone much further than SARA because we use an 8-step Intensive Engagement problem-solving process that incorporates SARA and a lot more. SARA stands for Scanning, Analysis, Response, and Assessment.

You should be familiar with the problem-solving methodologies that the police utilise, because it's part of your research to get in. They're not testing you to see whether you'll be able to deal with some firearms incident or something involving major disorder in the city that you're working in. That's the job of senior officers and officers with a lot more experience than you, but what they're looking for is to see whether you've done your research into those sorts of issues, the sorts of challenges that the police have now, and how they go about dealing with them. All those things I've just discussed are all publicly available for you.

So, like I said before, in your answers to all the above questions, you will first explain why it's so important that you, for example, challenge inappropriate behaviour. You'd explain how this will link in with the value of Integrity in the Competency and Values Framework as well as The Code of Ethics. Then you would explain how you would go about doing it. This is where you would describe how you think you would go about dealing with an issue. I would also include an example of what might be inappropriate behaviour to provide context. Next comes what, as in, what would this result in?

So, when you do these things they ask you about, you should be able to describe what the result be. How will it benefit members of the community? How will it benefit the police service?

That's how we use the, 'why, how, and the what' model for forward-facing questions. This might sound challenging now, but the more you practice this, the easier it will get. Like I said before, it's not something that most forces do, but there are enough who do now and might do in the future, for you to think about preparing for these types of questions. As I said before, Derbyshire Constabulary use Forward Facing questions as do Durham Constabulary (who ask you how you would go about doing problem-solving as a police officer).

I don't think you'd ever get asked more than one or two forward facing questions in an interview. Once you start getting into them, and you start practicing them, you'll be absolutely fine.

I can't think at this moment in time of any other questions that you would be asked at this stage of your potential career that are forward-facing. Once you're in the police and you're looking to get promoted to sergeant and inspector, yes, they do get more challenging, but for this moment in time, the questions I have outlined in this chapter, they're not going to be any more complicated than that.

If you do come across one that's more complicated than that, then please do let me know and I'll make it an addition to this book.

https://bluelightonline.co.uk/book

Chapter 17 - Sample Final Interview Questions!

In this chapter, we're going to build on the one where we looked at how we're going to structure the answers to our final interview questions, especially the ones that start off with, 'please, can you tell me about a time when....?' As a reminder, these are sort of questions that explore your previous experiences and assess them against the behaviours required of you as a police officer from The Competency and Values Framework.

Now, as I've said before, this isn't about, 'knowing your competencies,' and it's not about reeling off a load of buzzwords from The Competency and Values Framework.

What I'm going to do in this chapter is to give you a sample set of questions that you could get asked. I'm going to give you two out of the four values and two out of the six competencies. If you'd like to find out more, if you'd like to see all my question banks, the same ones that have helped 1000's of my clients over the past decade to succeed, then go to the Offer Wall at the end of this chapter (the Platinum package). At the end of every chapter, you'll see some amazing offers to work personally with me, where you'll not only get a full question bank, but also the opportunity to practice with me in my workshops. That's the thing that really guarantees a pass.

So anyway, to the questions that you are going to be asked. I'm not going to guarantee that you're definitely going to be asked these questions, but these are the sort of questions that commonly get asked.

Impartiality Value

We're going to start with the value of Impartiality. So, the question could be:

'Please can you tell me about a time when you had to deal with a conflict situation or a difficult situation that required you to mediate between two people?'

It could be phrased like that or:

'Please can you tell me about a time when you had to deal with a conflict situation?'

Or:

'Please can you tell me about a time when you had to deal with a situation where you've had some mediate between others or to help others come to a common understanding?'

This is quite a tough question.

Now, you know from the previous chapter the structure to use, but what about the content? What they do not want to hear about is how you approached this from the physical conflict perspective. They're looking for how you've managed a disagreement between you and another person or between two people. Physical conflicts are not going to enable you to demonstrate the supplementary points. And remember these supplementary points are from the behaviours within the value in The Competency and Values Framework. As well as predicting the questions, one of the other things I've done is to turn the behaviours into plain English as opposed to 'Competency Speak,' so you can understand them. So, when you answer the question, you should include as many of the following points as possible. These points will form the basis, by the way, of the marking guide that Forces use:

How did you take into account the needs of the other person(s)?

How did you ensure that the actions you took or proposed were fair?

How did you ensure that the other person(s) had an opportunity to express their views?

How do you ensure that you are consistent with your communication / message?

How did you go about ensuring that the other person(s) felt they were being listened to? (Think about the questions you were asked, or the comments made, and how you made a note of them or used active listening to reflect to your understanding)

How did you ensure that your decision was fair?

So, there you go folks. Impartiality is the first value.

Integrity Value

We're now going to move on to the next value of Integrity. I can pretty much guarantee you're going to get asked questions around this, which could be:

'Please, can you tell me about a time when you've done the right thing even when a different option would have been easier?'

Or:

'Please, can you tell me about a time when you've challenged inappropriate behaviour or actions?'

Now, the key point here is they are not looking for you to challenge the inappropriate behaviour or actions of, for example, a customer or if you're a Special Constable, someone out on the streets at 11 o'clock at night who is shouting, screaming, and swearing. When you look at the actual value itself in the CVF, it talks about challenging the inappropriate behaviour of colleagues. So, if you've got an example where you've challenged an inappropriate behaviour of a colleague, you've got a far stronger answer. However, you might be thinking, 'I've not had that opportunity yet.' Oh, yes you have! Please don't try to persuade me that throughout your life, there's not been an opportunity to challenge a colleague, or a fellow student, or someone who volunteers with you. It doesn't have to be sexism or racism; it could just be someone not following policy or someone taking an inappropriate shortcut in what they are doing.

To help you, here's a good example provided in a 1-2-1 session with a recent client.

She was a manager at a restaurant and saw how a fellow manager was inputting less money than they should have into the till so that they could keep a larger proportion of the tip for themselves. After observing this she made sure that what she saw was correct by checking the till receipts against the actual invoice presented to the customer. She also checked the internal CCTV and looked up what the contractual agreement was for members of staff around any dishonest actions.

She went on to challenge the individual who became angry with her. From there she reported the matter to the directors of the business and after presenting her evidence, her colleague was dismissed.

There was a lot more she discussed: impact; options; how she carried out the challenge; how she kept her emotions in check; how she managed the fall out with the rest of the team and a lot more. It was an awesome answer, and it got her (together with her other answers) a really high mark at her interview. Her interviewers called her the next day to say so!

So, you will have had the opportunity to challenge inappropriate behaviour, but you might not have viewed it as such. If you haven't done this yet, now is the time to start thinking, 'well, I need to almost engineer this happen. I need to wait for someone to do something inappropriate, and then I'm going to challenge them.' Just to add, challenging another person is not always about getting people into trouble. It can be about supporting people and helping people, because a lot of the time when people do something called 'inappropriate behaviour,' it's because they either don't know, it's inappropriate, or they've got some other reasons like a welfare issue.

When you deal with this kind of issue you are demonstrating you have the value of integrity, which for me means:

Doing the right thing in difficult or challenging circumstances, even if no one is watching you.

So, for the supplementary points, which will form the basis of the marking guide:

What guidelines, advice or policy did you refer to and how did you source that information?

What consideration did you give to the reputation of the organisation you are part of?

How did you ensure that you weren't overbearing or disrespectful of others?

These behavioural statements will probably form part of the marking guide. Now, let's move on to some of the competencies.

We are Emotionally Aware Competency

HOW TO SUCCEED IN THE POLICE RECRUITMENT PROCESS

Let's look at, We are Emotionally Aware. This is an interesting one as the questions can vary - I've got quite a few examples in my question bank, but let's look at this one. This is a popular one in police circles. This one's been asked on so many specialist post interviews I've run as a police officer interviewing other police officers for. It also gets asked on promotion boards and I know it also gets asked at force final interviews as well.

The question is:

'Please, can you tell me about a time when you have changed the style of your approach or communication to meet the needs someone else's needs?'

What you should be thinking about here is Protected Characteristics: cultural issues; religious issues; race; sexual orientation; marital status and beliefs.

This question is all about equality. Some of you might be thinking, and I've heard people say this on my webinars and practice sessions, how, 'equality is about treating people equally.' No, it isn't. Equality is about treating people according to their needs.

So, this is what this one is about. How do you treat people according to their needs? So, to the supplementary points, quite a few of them here:

How did you treat the other person with respect, tolerance, and compassion?

How did you seek to understand another person's perspective, values, or beliefs?

How did you remain calm?

How did you control your own emotions?

How did you deal with any stress or pressure?

How did you ask for support if it was required?

How did you go about understanding the other person's beliefs or values? (Think here about asking them questions. That's the best way of understanding other people's beliefs or values, to ask them questions. What questions did you ask them?)

How did you ensure that your communication was clear and simple so it could be understood by others?

How did you go about trying to understand the thoughts and concerns of others, even when they couldn't express themselves clearly? (This is about the open questions you used or how you asked those open questions in a different way for people who might be confused or vulnerable for some reason and just can't explain their thoughts and concerns. How did you go about trying to understand them?)

So, there are quite a lot of supplementary points there - if you can include as many of those as possible in your answer, then you will be awesome.

So, let's look at the next competency.

We Deliver Support and Inspire Competency

The question is unlikely to be, 'please can you tell me about a time when you've inspired someone else?' When you look at the behaviours in this competency, it's about something else. It's not quite about Deliver, Support, and Inspire. They should have called it something else. I'm not quite sure what, but they should have called it something else.

So, I'll give you a couple of sample questions here:

'Please can you tell me about a time when you've taken on a challenging task?'

'Please can you tell me about a time when you have worked on a task to a challenging deadline or under pressure?' (They want you to talk about how you prioritised, how you looked at importance and urgency, and how you prioritised based on that).

'Please can you tell me about a time when you've had to overcome an obstacle in order to achieve something?

That last question is an interesting one - I've just covered it on a 1-2-1 with one of my clients who is preparing for their final interview. Before they came to me, they'd failed their final interview for their chosen force, and this was one of the questions that he failed on:

'Please can you tell me about a time when you've had to overcome obstacles in order to achieve an outcome?'

So, the supplementary points here, which are going to form part of the marking guide. Remember, all these supplementary points are from the behaviours within the competency:

How did you know that your efforts contributed to the organisation's aim?

How did you ensure that what you were doing was both efficient and effective?

How did you deal with any obstacles? How do you keep up with any organisational or external changes?

To what extent did other people see you as a role model?

How did you develop yourself as a role model?

So, there you go. Some quite challenging behaviours for you to include in your answer. If you think about the role model part, there's no point in deciding, 'I'm going to be a role model and demonstrate the sort of behaviours expected of police officers when I apply to join the police.' You should be doing this now. Okay? You should be demonstrating all the behaviours expected of you now!

So, one of the things you should be doing a lot of is demonstrating all the behaviours from the Competency and Values Framework in the 'here and now,' not just waiting until you apply to join the police. This requires you to really step up to the plate, because it's not easy to be a role model. Sometimes it's easier just to go along with the flow and to go along with what other people are doing. It's far harder to be that role model. So, how did you develop yourself as a role model, and to what extent do they see you as a role model? This is a really important part of Deliver, Support and Inspire.

So, there you go, folks. I hope you've found these sample questions useful. Other competencies to prepare answers for are:

We Analyse Critically

We are Collaborative

We take Ownership

We are Innovative and Open-Minded

We also have two more values in the question bank:

Public Service

Transparency

One of the things I urge you to do folks is to join the interview course, access that question bank, and start practicing. First, write down your answers and start framing them around the SAARLKU model I have already provided you with.

And then start practicing.

The best thing you can start doing now is starting to practice. Just practice, start practicing now and practice every day. Take some action every day that's going to take you closer and closer to how you want to come across in your interview. As someone who is authentic, emotional, structured, and has a detailed approach. You are interesting to listen to and you show potential. That's what we do in my practice sessions – I help build up your confidence, so you don't sound rehearsed and that's only going to come through practice.

So, folks. I hope you've enjoyed this and got a lot out of it. I look forward to seeing you on one of my webinars.

https://bluelightonline.co.uk/book

Chapter 18 - Direct Entry Detective Assessments

In this chapter, we're going to take a look at the sort of exercises you might expect if you're going for direct entry detective. Currently the Metropolitan Police use an in-tray and a briefing exercise. So, what I'm going to do in this chapter is to give you an introduction on how to deal with both of those exercises, as well as an idea of who to approach the exercises other forces set.

Of course, if you want even more detail, the templates, the worksheets, and the explainer videos, then those are all in the online interview course. You'll find those under the Platinum package in the Offer Wall, which you have as part of this book (end of every chapter).

But for many of you, the guidance in this chapter might just suffice.

The In-Tray Exercise

So, for the in-tray exercise, what they're going to give you is a series of small conundrums that you've got to think about in terms of urgency and importance as well as how you would action it.

Is it you that's going to deal with it?

And do you need to deal with it now?

Or is it something that could be diarised for you to deal with it later?

Or is it something that is urgent? It needs dealing with today. But it doesn't need dealing with by you?

What sort of actions would you take to deal with that conundrum?

So, what sort of problems are they going to give you? It could be something like someone who is going to attend the police station in two hours' time who is a victim of a historical sexual assault. They came in yesterday, but there was no one available and your sergeant has booked you in to see them today. They might ask how you would go about dealing with this, but they might also create something else that conflicts with that. So, you've got to decide which of those things is more important and give you a rationale for your decision. And for the things that aren't as important, how you going to delegate them.

So that's what I think the entire exercise is going to be made up of. They're going to give you a lot of information, they're going to overload you with information! The way to deal with this exercise is by coming up with a structured plan where you have prioritised everything in respect of urgency and importance. For any of you who watch my YouTube videos and listen to my podcasts (you don't? Check out the Offer Wall at the end of the chapter for the links) you might be thinking, 'isn't Brendan talking about the Eisenhower Matrix here?'

U.S. President Eisenhower once said:

What is important is seldom urgent, and what is urgent is seldom important.

So, based on that phrase, we can come up with a matrix we can use for this exercise. If we take a rectangle and turn it into four rectangles by drawing a line horizontally and one vertically. Through that rectangle, we get four squares (or smaller rectangles).

In the top left-hand square, you're going to have what is important and urgent. So, these are the things that need dealing with by you because they are important (if it is important, it means you need to deal with it) and today in the here and now because they are also urgent. But everything can't be a priority, because if everything is a priority, nothing is. So, you've got to decide which things are important and need dealing with by you now. All these issues and problems go in the top left-hand square.

Next, we go to the top right-hand square. These are the things that are important, they need dealing with by you, but they're not urgent, so you can diarise them for another day. But when that other day comes, suddenly they become important and urgent. So, they move into a different box (top left-hand square, urgent and important).

In the bottom left-hand corner, you've got things that are urgent but they're not important. So, they don't need dealing with by you, but they need dealing with by someone today. So, these are things that you can delegate to others. In my online course, and in my webinars, I explain about how you go about building up the relationships which will enable you to delegate things to other people. Despite the fact that you are a detective constable, as a DC, there are going to be a lot of things that you need to delegate to others and there are ways of doing that in a way that will ensure people do what you ask them to.

Now the bottom right-hand square is for the things that aren't urgent and aren't important, but that's not to say that you shouldn't refer those things to someone else. They might not be urgent, and might not be important to you, but they might be to someone else. These are the things that you pass on to other people to deal with, but do not expect an update or any other reports being made back to you.

An example of that would be a scenario where maybe an 85-year-old vulnerable person is suffering from Anti-social Behaviour, where children on the street are kicking a ball against the side of their house and it's causing them to lose sleep. She's very worried about it as she challenged them recently, but they told her to, 'F*£k off.'

Now that clearly needs dealing with, but it's got nothing to do with your role as a detective. How it even ends up on your desk is beyond me, but if something like that does end up on your desk, then you need to be able to rationalise why it's not urgent for you, and it's not important to you, but it might be something that needs dealing with in 'here and now' by the Neighbourhood Team. So, you task it up for the Neighbourhood Team to deal with, and you wouldn't expect them to reply. Does that make sense?

So in terms of that urgency, you can also think about things like, threat, harm, and risk. So, what or who is the threat? And if that threat were to appear, what potential harm could it cause to someone? And, what's the risk of it happening? You can also use threat, harm, and risk as a way of determining the urgency of something. So, there you go. That's how you deal with the in-tray exercise.

If you'd like to have a go at an in-tray exercise, there's a practice exercise in the interview course. With the Platinum Interview Course package, you'll also get access to interactive webinars where we practice this kind of thing as well as recordings of previous webinars. Check out the Offer Wall at the end of this chapter.

The Briefing Exercise

When it comes to the Briefing exercise, my best guess is that they're going to give you a scenario to deal with that is more than just a couple of burglaries. It will probably be something to do with a violent crime that's taken place, a serious assault. There will be a certain street it's taken part on, and nearby there'll be some evidence, maybe a baseball bat that's been used. However, this could also be something that was potentially used, you won't know from the information provided. There might also be something that's been potentially discarded, which could be evidence of someone's identity - someone who could be involved. Your victim is unconscious and can't tell you anything. They'll also give you a load more information about the incident: the times; the locations where connecting parts of the incident occurred; a couple of incident logs and some conflicting information.

If all of this makes you feel overloaded, then that's what the exercise will feel like. It won't be straight forward; it's been designed to confuse and disorientate you. You job is to make sense of it all and deliver a 10-minute briefing to a real-life detective sergeant or inspector.

You will be given some time to prepare for the 10-minute briefing, but not nearly enough as they want to see how you manage pressure. The way that's going to work from there – you'll enter a room where you'll meet the detective sergeant or inspector, they're going to welcome you into the room, sit you down, sit back and go, 'right, off you go, you've got ten minutes.' At that point, you're on your own, and they're going to expect a structured and detailed briefing from you.

Now, I think this is unfair on people who've never had any kind of contact with the police or don't really know how these things work. If you're a PCSO or Special Constable who has been witness to briefings or might have been part of a briefing, you have a big advantage. But if you've never seen one before you wouldn't know what to do to prepare.

HOW TO SUCCEED IN THE POLICE RECRUITMENT PROCESS

This is why I'm going to introduce you to a briefing model called IIMARCH.

IIMARCH is a well-recognised briefing and debriefing model within the policing and emergency services world, and it's something that all detectives in every force will be aware of. When you deliver a briefing, in the style of IIMARCH, you're going to have a Detective Sergeant or Detective Inspector in front of you, who's doing the assessing thinking, 'this person has been so coached by someone who is 'Job.' Whether you have been coached or not, it doesn't matter, you'll hit all of what they are looking for on the marking guide. However, they wouldn't normally expect a candidate to be so familiar with the IIMARCH methodology.

IIMARCH stands for:

Information

Intention

Method

Administration

Risk

Communication

Health and Safety / Human Rights

So, broken down into more detail for you.

Information

First, at the information stage, you'll be wanting to '5 WH' it. So, you'll use your 5 WH skills to ask questions of the incident.

What time did it occur?

Where did it occur?

And as we do 5 WH in a simple to complex way – the first questions are the simpler ones, and then they get more complex.

What happened?

Who was involved?

How did they carry out the offence?

What caused them to do it?

Why did it happen?

What's the impact on the community going to be?

We're going to have lots of five 5 WH questions, so that you can deliver information about the incident using a timeline. A timeline is probably the best way of presenting all the information so that it appears to flow.

Moreover, you'll be wanting to think about not just what you know, but also what you don't know. This is important. What don't you know, and how are you going to go about securing the information about the things you don't know?

Now, you might be thinking, 'I don't know what I don't know.' I'll give you some ideas: things like:

Who are the other individuals involved, the other possible offenders?

How many?

Who are they?

What vehicles were involved?

What direction did they go in?

There will be lots of things like that which aren't known.

You'll be expected to be able to interrogate the actual pack that they give you for the things that aren't known at this time. It's important you mention these things as what you don't know creates lines of enquiry. This then leads to the next stage, the intention.

Intention

Now, most people would probably go straight into how the intention is to catch the people who've committed the crime. However, this is the last thing to mention!

They will be expecting you to use the 'Five Pillars of Investigative Doctrine.' To find this go to the College of Policing website where you'll find the Investigative Doctrine Authorised Professional Practice. On my Interview course (see the Platinum Package in the Offer Wall at the end of this chapter) we utilise the Authorised Professional Practice to build up a really, really detailed model for IIMARCH. What you're getting here is just a bit of a foundation.

So, the 'Five Pillars' of an investigation go in this order:

Preserving life

Preserving the scene

Preserving and securing evidence

Identifying victims and witnesses

Identifying the suspect

So, you see, if you try and identify a suspect and go chasing the suspect when your scene hasn't been secured and where your evidence is not being preserved and secured, you'll have a great suspect, but no evidence. So that's why it goes in that order and that's the way of thinking that you should adopt. Unless, of course, the suspect is staring you in the face, in which case you're going to get them arrested! You don't need to wait to do all the other things first!

Method

Now we come to the Method stage. Here you will explain how you're going to follow up on the lines of inquiry and how you're going to utilise passive evidence sources such as ANPR. You'll also mention any 'phone work' that needs doing – mobile phones leave behind an incredible evidence trail, Get the phones seized and examined.

Administration

Administration - this is quite a big one. You'd be looking at what the command structure is, what procedure you're going to utilise for arrests or searches, who's going to be doing the house-to-house, this is the 'how' in respect of what everyone is going to do. There's a lot to the Administration stage, and you'll be talking about how you're going to take command and control of all of it.
Risk

In terms of risk, in the Interview Course we look at a matrix where we utilise threat, harm, and risk. So, where's the threat coming from, is it a continuous threat? If that threat were to happen, what potential harm would come to people? Who would those people be? What's the risk of that harm happening? Talking about threat, harm, and risk in your briefing will add some serious marks to your efforts!

Communication

Moving into the Communication stage – this looks at how you're going to communicate with all the people involved. Having an 'if asked' message is also important, so when people like members of community ask, 'what's happened here?' they are getting a consistent message. You'll also explain how you would deal with things like social media, and the press.

Health and Safety / Human Rights

Last part, Health and Safety. What needs to be done to ensure that our officers and everyone involved in the investigation are safe? The 'H' can also mean Human Rights. This where you should be considering things like Section 60 search authorisations. So, if there's been a violent crime and weapons have been used, you might be looking at an authorisation for a Section 60, which is pretty much a blanket approach to stop and search where you don't need 'reasonable grounds to believe' to be able to search people. But then this has a Human Rights impact on the community, you'll be wanting to lift that as soon as is practicable.

So, there you go, there's an introduction into the Briefing Exercise. There's a lot more to it though, a lot more, and to cover all of what you need to do to prepare would be far more than one chapter. This would probably be a book in itself! What is in this chapter is just to give you a foundation and for many of you this will be enough. The models and structured approaches explained so far are what I would advocate for any force that uses briefings and prioritisation exercises.

However, some forces might also ask you to do a presentation as well / instead.

Presentations made up of several specific questions that are provided beforehand aren't really presentations, think of them as several interview questions, all wrapped up into one big set of answers. What tends to happen when my clients hear they must do a presentation is for them to go into panic mode as, 'I'm no good at doing presentations!'

Reframe what the force is telling you to do into, 'here are the interview questions we are going to ask you,' and suddenly the challenge doesn't quite seem so daunting?

Even if they give you a single topic like, 'The impact of knife crime,' or, 'how organised crime is impacting on our communities,' it's still just one big interview question and you will only have a maximum of 10 minutes to deliver your 'answer.' 10 minutes will fly by, it really will. So, my top tip is to avoid the over wordy PowerPoint presentation you might be thinking of doing. Use props, yes, but do not use PowerPoint.

Why? Well, when was the last time you ever went to a PowerPoint presentation that was fascinating? When was the last time you ever heard anyone walking out of a room saying, 'that was an awesome Power Point presentation. I so enjoyed it.' Never? So, whatever you do, don't bore them with one. There are ways of using props in any presentation, and if it's just 10 minutes, it's not a long time. By the time, you've done your introduction, tell them what you're going to tell them and then told them what you're going to tell them, and then reviewed what you've told them, that's it, 10 minutes is up. It flies by, honestly, it flies by.

https://bluelightonline.co.uk/book

Conclusion - So, how did you find this book?

My aim was to provide you with the best foundation possible to take you from the point where you are thinking about joining the police, all the way to the point where you are walking through the doors of your chosen police force HQ!

I hope I succeeded in this aim!

However, it is just a book, and can be no substitute for practice, but at least you now know what you need to practice!

I do hope you will come and join me in the online courses and practice webinars that go with them.

The online courses provide far, far more detail through templates, question banks, exercises, and explainer videos. The online courses are the knowledge and understanding, the webinars are where you get to put it all into practice.

For some of you, the contents of this book will be enough to get you through. If that is the case, then I will be so pleased for you, please do drop me a line info@bluelightconsultancy.com to let me know.

For the rest of you, I hope to see you on my webinars, where I will guarantee you a pass in your online assessment centre or at your final / in-force / senior interview.

Yes, you heard that right, a guarantee!

I'm all in on this journey with you, I'll show you the way, you just have to do the hard work. And if you do all that hard work and you still do not pass, I will provide you with a full refund (subject to sensible T&C like, you have to have done the work!!)

So, the question to ask yourself is, am I ready to put in that kind of commitment? The hard work that will guarantee me a pass for my dream career?

I'm all in on this journey, are you?

If the answer is yes, then look at the Offer Wall at the end of this and every other chapter in this book. That is where you will find offers on my online course plus webinar packages you won't find anywhere else. They are exclusively for you as a way of saying 'Thank You' for joining me so far on this journey.

And for that moment when you get a start date?

The journey is far from over! This is where you get to the real starting line!

This is where you will discover all the other career support I provide for serving officers. Ask to join the free Bluelight Police In-Service Development Cadre (you will find this in Facebook Groups) and watch out for future Bluelight publications on how to create your successful and fulfilling career!

To your success!

Brendan

About the author

Brendan O'Brien spent three decades as a police officer in The Cheshire Constabulary, Bermuda Police and in Greater Manchester Police, where he retired as an inspector (that's Brendan on the front cover with the red epaulettes!). During that time he served in a range of roles: Response; Staff Officer; Detective; Custody Officer; Specialist Training; Special Branch; Neighbourhood Inspector and HQ Change Branch.

Since retiring, Brendan has continued to serve through his business, Bluelight Consultancy, as: an Approved Provider to deliver qualifications from The College of Policing; an International Advisory Board member for European Union Community Policing projects and as an Associate in The College of Policing's Organisational Development Unit. He continues to support Forces as an advisor in Police Recruitment and in improving their Problem Solving / Community Policing capability. Brendan has also spoken at several Policing Conferences in the United Kingdom, Hungary and Germany.

Brendan is a qualified Police Trainer and Trainer of Trainers and holds a Masters in Education in Training and Personnel Evaluation.

You can find out more about Brendan's work and how it can help to guarantee a pass in the Police Recruitment Process at
www.bluelightonline.co.uk

Printed in Great Britain
by Amazon